ALRIGHT
ALDO

ALRIGHT ALDO

Sport Media

To my friends and rivals in the
game, without whom football
would not be the same.

To my family – Joan, Paul,
Joanne, my grandson Jamie,
my mum and my late dad,
not forgetting the Liverpool
and Ireland family.

And, as always, to the 96.
Never far from my thoughts.

John Aldridge

Sport Media

Copyright: John Aldridge

Produced in 2010 by Trinity Mirror Sport Media:

Business Development Director: Mark Dickinson. Executive Editor: Ken Rogers.
Senior Editor: Steve Hanrahan. Editor: Paul Dove. Senior Art Editor: Rick Cooke.
Sales and Marketing Manager: Elizabeth Morgan.
Sales and Marketing Assistant: Karen Cadman.
Marketing Executive: Claire Brown.

Cover design: Lee Ashun.
Additional design: Alison Gilliland, Matthew Barnes, Lee Ashun.
Additional proofing: Michael McGuinness.

ISBN: 9781906802585

Photographs:

Trinity Mirror, PA Pics, John Aldridge collection.
Material has been used courtesy of John Aldridge. Every effort has been made by the publisher to
establish the copyright of images/material included in this book. The publisher will guarantee that any
inaccuracies or omissions of which they are made aware will be rectified in future editions.
LFC Weekly Magazine: Copyright Liverpool Football Club.

Printed and bound in the UK by CPI Mackays, Chatham ME5 8TD

Liverpool FC is hard as hell
United, Tottenham, Arsenal
Watch my lips, and I will spell
'cause they don't just play,
but they can rap as well
Liverpool FC
Liverpool FC

My idea was to build Liverpool
into a bastion of invincibility...
Napoleon had that idea he'd
have conquered the bloody world
Walk on... walk on... with hope...
in your heart...
and you'll never walk... alone

Alright Aldo
Sound as a pound
I'm cushty la but there's nothing down

The rest of the lads ain't got it sussed
We'll have to learn 'em to talk like us...

The Anfield Rap

POST-WAR TOP GOALSCORERS
(Who have played in the English league)

Name	Total goals
John Aldridge	476
Jimmy Greaves	475*
Arthur Rowley	464
Alan Shearer	422**

* Includes two Charity Shield goals
** Includes England Under-21 goals

Statistics by Dave Ball

'I consider him not just a player for me but a great friend as well. We have had some great times together, drank the odd pub dry, sang a song or two and above all, enjoyed the Irish. Give me a ring John and I will take you salmon fishing now we have time'.

**Jack Charlton,
former Republic of Ireland manager**

'Alright Aldo, sound as a pound, I'm cushty la but there's nothing down... These are just a few words from our smash hit, can you remember it? Sorry I can't be there tonight but you deserve everything you get. You're a great lad but a crap manager!'

**Steve McMahon,
ex-rival boss of Tranmere
& former Anfield team-mate**

'Sorry I am not able to attend but I am in very serious preparation for the Roy Castle game at Anfield tomorrow, unlike you. I hope you are not going to indulge in any unforeseen preparation, although I think that was your normal preparation for a Liverpool match!'

**Kenny Dalglish,
former Liverpool manager**

(Tongue-in-cheek messages sent to Aldo before a Variety Club tribute dinner, May 1998, when he retired as a player)

MATCH DAY...

"Aldo is usually late," Radio City commentator Steve Hothersall informs us with a chuckle. "I'll get a text from him saying make the departure time 20 past rather than ten past. He never wants to get to the ground too early."

He will soon celebrate 10 years as a media pundit but the man who scored 63 goals in 104 Liverpool appearances and still enjoys legendary status on the Kop can enjoy that luxury.

For his colleague the day is more demanding. He likes to spend at least two hours in the iconic Radio City tower in the heart of Liverpool swotting up for the broadcast ahead.

Research done, sports pages of the newspapers scanned and broadcasting equipment collected, an extra layer of clothing is grabbed. Despite the fact the time is still before midday, it's already freezing outside and will surely get even colder before the action kicks off at 3pm.

Descending from the top of St. John's Beacon is an ear-popping experience. The time required for the lift to drop to the bottom is a reminder of how high you have just been. It's an even longer journey back up when you've forgotten the car keys.

The hustle and bustle of pre-Christmas shoppers means we have to patiently exit the multi-storey car park that adjoins St John's shopping centre before we go on our way to Lancashire via collecting Aldo.

"Me and John are great friends," Hothersall explains as the

Radio City car progresses through the Saturday traffic. "But we do argue like a married couple; you'll see that today."

A quick pit-stop at a petrol station acquires a pre-requested bottle of water for Aldo before we reach the former Tranmere manager's home. The front door is already open and he briefly appears before shouting something incomprehensible and disappearing again.

Ten minutes later Aldo walks down the short driveway and jumps into the passenger seat. Straight away he's chatting about football in the same passionate way he does on the radio. That's why supporters love to hear him on air – he's passionate and he's honest.

Liverpool are at Blackburn Rovers today. After a quick glance at the dashboard clock, Aldo states that we will reach the ground far too early. Steve isn't so sure. "No, there will be plenty of traffic along the A666," he replies.

"I'm telling you we'll be in there by quarter past one," Aldo counters. "No, it'll be at least 25 past by the time we get from the car to the ground, grab our tickets and then go up to the press room," Hothersall insists.

Aldo isn't convinced. He's shaking his head. "I'll put £20 on us being in there too early," he says with an outstretched hand. The wager is politely refused as the pair laugh about it.

"Look at the state of them idiots," Aldo comments as two Blackburn fans dressed as Big Bird and Elmo from Sesame Street walk along.

Steve has to drive quicker as we go past a huge crowd of travelling fans outside one of the local watering holes. Such is the former number eight's popularity amongst Kopites that if he's spotted in the car we could be here all day waiting for him to sign autographs. We've arrived in Blackburn and park up before making the short walk to the stadium.

"You should put your boots on today John," a supporter shouts as we stroll along. Another shakes his hand before a carload of fans gives him a cheer.

Even the ladies at reception are happy to see Aldo as he greets them with a smile.

Hothersall immediately heads up to the press box to get set up while Aldo goes to the pressroom. The clock says 1.20pm.

With Hothersall being a vegetarian he's asked Aldo to check if there is anything on the menu which will take his fancy. The expected Lancashire hotpot is not available. Instead it's bangers and mash doused in gravy. Grub served, Aldo takes a seat and begins to dig in. As he does the sound of loud tapping on a laptop can be heard from the corner. The source of the noise is a bespectacled Stan Collymore.

"You writing your Christmas card list Stan?" Aldo asks.

A game live on the TV is a good way of killing the waiting time until the radio broadcast begins at 2pm. Another method he uses to kill the boredom is a pre-game flutter.

"Usually £20 on Stevie to score first or last. I won a few quid on that last season. I don't think I'll put anything on today," Aldo wisely decides.

Hothersall starts the Radio City coverage by revealing that Steven Gerrard scored his first senior goal 10 years ago today in a 4-1 win over Sheffield Wednesday. It would be just like the skipper to mark his 500th appearance with another strike. Maybe Aldo is now regretting not having that bet.

On the field a quiet opening 20 minutes is livened up by some quick-witted punditry. With Rovers sponsored by Crown Paints the name appears at regular intervals on the flashy modern advertising boards at the side of the pitch. When it pops up again for the umpteenth time Aldo is straight in. "It's suitable because so far this has been like watching paint dry!"

Halfway through the first period the broadcast unexpectedly ceases. "Gremlins" is the official explanation before normal service quickly returns. It's later revealed the cause is Aldo's knee accidentally disconnecting a wire.

The whistle goes and it's back downstairs to the warmth of the pressroom for Aldo. In freezing conditions the hacks slurp down the half-time soup on offer. Aldo brings some back upstairs for the second half.

A lively start, especially when compared to what has gone before, results in the Reds appealing for a penalty before the name of former red El Hadji Diouf enters the referee's notebook. "What an idiot" Aldo states. Despite a promising start to the second half, however, the game peters out into a 0-0 draw.

Aldo takes off his headphones and heads for the comfort of the pressroom. Following a cuppa he is soon back in his seat for the football phone-in. Over the past decade it has become a matchday institution, as essential a part of the experience for some as a pre-match pint, a pie and a programme.

The stadium is now deserted apart from some players going through the motions of a post-match warmdown and some stewards performing the last of the day's tasks. Behind the scenes, an army of staff works busily to restore the ground to its former condition.

While all this is going on, Liverpool fans are filing back to their cars and coaches in the rain, preparing to tune in to the radio as they head home trying to come to terms with the disappointment of a couple of points lost. After such a frustrating afternoon on the pitch, it isn't long before the monitor lights up with the first caller.

"Who would you like to talk to?" asks Steve Hothersall.

It is Bob from Liverpool. He hasn't been to the game but says he would like to talk about the Reds. There is a short pause then the caller starts to make his point.

"Alright Aldo..."

And so it begins.

**JOHN HYNES,
LFC WEEKLY MAGAZINE, 2009**

TWO MONTHS LATER...

It's 12.30pm on a Sunday and there's a knock at my door.

I can't believe that's my mate Steve Hothersall already.

Today we're going to Manchester City to cover Liverpool's game in the Premier League for the local radio station, Radio City. The City of Manchester stadium is only about 45 minutes away in the car on a good day and we don't kick off until 4pm but already Hothersall's here. He's an absolute stickler for getting there nice and early so we can get set up our equipment and get ready to cover the match.

Joining me for the first time is journalist John Hynes – like me a fellow Kopite and proud Irishman. Over the course of the season, we wrote this book together which takes you on quite a journey.

From early days at South Liverpool and Newport through to Oxford and making it at Liverpool before a spell in Spain and back to Merseyside with Tranmere, with an appearance or two for Ireland in between all that. I was lucky enough to get around quite a bit during my career.

I'll be telling you a few tales from those days plus also giving you an opinion or two along the way about the game as I see it now – especially about the team that we all love – Liverpool FC.

Hope you all enjoy the trip...

JOHN ALDRIDGE, 2010

Acknowledgements

Thanks to John and all at Trinity Mirror Sport Media
for their help with this book.

Thanks also to Radio City and to dedicated
statisticians Ged Rea and Dave Ball for researching
the facts and figures that set the record straight
about how many goals I scored during
the course of my career.

John Aldridge

About the co-author

Aldo wrote this book with John Hynes.
John is a writer for Trinity Mirror Sport Media,
publishers of the official Liverpool Football Club matchday
programme and LFC Weekly Magazine.

Last year John wrote The Irish Kop, an official
club book celebrating the famous link between
Liverpool FC and Ireland. He was born in Ireland and lives
in Liverpool. He is a lifelong Kopite.

ALRIGHT
ALDO
ON THE ROAD

TALKING FOOTBALL

'I'm tempted to say that Aldo's greatest ever performance for Liverpool was his commentary in Istanbul. It just summed up the passion of the man'
— Kevin Sampson, writer

'If anyone is in any doubt about what John Aldridge means to Liverpool fans then you just had to be at the airport after the European Cup final in Istanbul. Aldridge was mobbed by about 300 Liverpool fans and paraded around the airport on their shoulders as they sang Liverpool songs'
— Tony Barrett, The Times

Here's my press ticket for Istanbul. I'm sure every Liverpool fan who was lucky enough to be there on that unforgettable night has kept his ticket. I'm no different...

A MATTER OF OPINION

Steve Hothersall: Shevchenko... scored the winner two years ago... he's up against Dudek... will he hand Liverpool the European Cup?

(Short pause as Dudek saves the penalty)

Aldo: Yeeeeeeeeeeeeeeeeeeessssss... yeeeeeessss!
(High pitched scream continues)

No guesses for spotting which match I'm commentating on here. The amazing Champions League final of 2005 in Istanbul provided me with probably my best footballing experience since I pulled on the famous red shirt all those years ago.

I lost it big time when Jerzy Dudek saved that Shevchenko penalty and Liverpool won the European Cup for a fifth time. My colleague Steve Hothersall was left to do the talking while I joined in the celebrations. And I make no apologies for that!

I didn't imagine I'd experience such an unbelievable high when I agreed to take on the job of being an Anfield pundit with the local radio station four years previously.

After I left Tranmere in March 2001 I wasn't really sure what my next step in life would be. Then Radio 5 Live asked me if I'd work for them on the UEFA Cup final against Alaves in Dortmund.

As you may remember, it was a sensational match to watch and a great game to be able to talk about. Fortunately we ended on the winning side in a nine-goal thriller, which gave us our third cup of a dramatic season. I really enjoyed the experience of being on the radio and I thought I could get used to it. It felt natural because I've always loved my football and, as I'm sure most people would agree, I've always been opinionated.

The lads at Radio City had obviously spotted that and at the start of the following season they asked me if I'd like to do some work with them.

Ian St. John had been the regular co-commentator before then, but he'd had problems with Gerard Houllier. He'd been referring to him as 'the Frenchman' on air and Houllier hadn't been happy with that.

When I was starting out I didn't want to become known as another Jimmy Hill or Eamon Dunphy, guys who seem to have a go at players all the time just for the sake of it. I have criticised plenty, but only if they've really deserved it.

I'm talking about players like Andriy Voronin and Philipp Degen. They should be nowhere near a Liverpool shirt, not even in their wildest dreams. It's obvious that some players will never come good. The only one in recent times who has really proved me wrong is Yossi Benayoun. He'd always been a decent footballer, but during his first year at Liverpool he didn't do a lot and I couldn't understand why. Eventually he did go on to show his quality before departing for Chelsea.

I felt comfortable giving my opinions too because I'd played for Liverpool, played in Spain and gone to a European Championships and two World Cups. I know what I'm talking about. Likewise for Ronnie Whelan. He was very vocal about Rafa Benitez and people criticised him for that. But Ronnie won everything with Liverpool so has a great insight.

Unfortunately a lot of pundits haven't done anything similar. Some of them can talk a great game but they have never played to any decent standard. I think that if you're an ex-pro who is a pundit and you want to have a go at top class internationals, it helps if you have been there and done it yourself. Otherwise it can sometimes sound wrong.

Stan Collymore is another pundit who can annoy me on occasions, but only because he's so loud. Sometimes when Stan's doing his phone-in and he's trying to get his point across, you can't hear yourself think.

Of course, having said that, football is all about opinion and everyone is entitled to have a say.

That's the great thing about our game. After any match you will hear fans talking about the rights and wrongs of what they have just seen. The phone lines will be buzzing with supporters wanting to put forward their views and you will see the letters pages of the local newspaper packed with fans' comments – especially when something has happened that they are unhappy about.

That's why working in the media can be so interesting, being right at the centre of what's going on and hearing what people think about our game.

MY NAME IN PRINT

I was ten years-old when I first spotted my name in the local paper. My primary school had become champions of Liverpool and I'd scored a load of goals along the way. Seeing my name in print gave me a great buzz. Since then my family have kept all the cuttings from my career. They're in a box somewhere in the loft. As I got older I used to read all the match reports, to see if I was getting any criticism. My stance was always if I was scoring goals they couldn't have a go at me. I usually did that so didn't get much stick.

When I was in Spain the press were very different to what I'd experienced previously. They were more in your face. Every day at the training ground they'd be there asking us questions.

Marca and AS were the two biggest papers and they'd give each player a mark for their performance. Back then, not many of the English papers did that. I found it unusual at first, especially when I noticed how much attention my team-mates paid to those little numbers.

The morning after each game everyone would be checking their score. That came before eating breakfast or anything else at the training ground.

Later, as a manager, I learned that I had to pay even closer attention to the press, especially when it came to transfer speculation.

POWER OF THE PRESS

Before I'd even started to work as a media pundit, I was driving into work for another day as manager of Tranmere Rovers in 1998 when something happened that stopped me in my tracks. *'Steve Simonsen is in talks with Everton'* the man on the radio announced.

I was manager of the football club and yet this was the first I'd heard about my young England Under-21 goalkeeper leaving. I went ballistic, phoned the station to find out where the story had come from and gave them loads of abuse for broadcasting it. Then I called the chairman and the shit really hit the fan.

That incident showed me just how powerful the media can be. They'd known about the deal before me and they were proved right because Steve eventually did join Walter Smith's team.

DEGEN AND 'BOLOKOV'

Anybody who knows me will find it hard to believe I'm not swearing on air all the time. It's easy to do as David Speedie, a good mate of mine, demonstrated a few years ago.

He was co-commentating on Radio City with Steve and right at the start of the show he replied to a question by saying "Fucking hell".

I have done it too, but only now and again. The 2006 FA Cup final at Cardiff was one of the first occasions.

Ronnie (Whelan) was working on it with us and we were doing a quiz before the game, me against him. He looked over my shoulder to see an answer and, live on air, I screamed at him: "You cheating bastard." I just completely forgot where we were.

I once used the expression: "That was a holocaustic performance." Thankfully nobody picked up on it. It was something I've heard a lot of people use in football down through the years. It refers to someone having a nightmare of a game, although it's not a word anyone should use in connection with football. Gary Gillespie said it a few days later on air and didn't get away with it, like me. People were phoning in complaining. Apparently they had to edit the whole show before it went out on air again.

I think the only time some of my comments led to complaints was during Euro 96 when I was working for RTE. Bulgaria's goalkeeper got hit between the legs with the ball and during the half-time analysis, I said he might have to change his name to Bolakov. I don't think RTE liked that, and I haven't done too much work for them since.

I also used the line 'Degen you fanny' – referring to Philipp Degen – during the 2009/10 season. Again, it was a football expression that was said out of pure frustration.

We'd often call someone a 'fanny merchant'. He's one of those guys who loves looking at himself. He should be out on a catwalk rather than a pitch. I'd said it under my breath but again it just shows you how careful you have to be when you're on the radio. You have to keep your feelings under control, although I think it's fine to cheer the team when things have gone well. I'm sure you will have heard me going mad on the radio when a Liverpool goal has gone in. There's nothing wrong with that.

AWAY DAYS

Working on the radio is enjoyable. There are some downsides too though, such as horrible long journeys to away games. Chelsea in the League Cup in December 2007 was probably the worst. As usual we set off early, probably the earliest ever, because it was a midweek game in London.

We never even made it near Stamford Bridge. There was an accident on the motorway that led to the worst tailback I've ever seen. Instead of waiting we turned back because we knew we couldn't get there for kick-off.

We got to watch it, though, in a dodgy pub in the middle of

Banbury in Oxfordshire, near where I used to live. It reminded me of The Jockey pub from Shameless. There was every kind of character in there from druggies to gangsters to scallies. It was horrible.

Liverpool, with Charles Itandje in goal, lost 2-0 and had Peter Crouch sent off so we weren't too bothered about not making it to the stadium in the end (and we still got a few bob for it, as usual).

A lot of the London grounds are really difficult to get to. I've never been a fan of Upton Park or Selhurst Park because it's almost impossible to find them and traffic in the capital is a nightmare. The Valley, Charlton Athletic's ground, was another that we've had huge trouble locating in recent years. One season we were late and just pulled up outside a few minutes before kick-off.

If we'd had to go looking for a parking space we'd have been there all day. Our only option was to blag our way into the car park. The attendant on duty was a bit naïve so Steve ended up giving him the old *"It's John Aldridge"* line and he let us pass.

We'd just got to our seats when our car registration was called out over the loudspeaker because we were causing an obstruction. Moving it wasn't an option because the game was starting. I spent the 90 minutes winding Steve up with jokes about the bomb squad dismantling his car outside.

After a long journey we need to eat, and usually have a pre-match meal in the pressroom. Some of the facilities are quite decent now but that wasn't the case at Portsmouth a couple of years ago. They used to put the press in a pre-fabricated building at the back of the stand which wasn't the best.

Most clubs in the Premier League do a decent feed now, though, especially Arsenal. They mightn't have won any trophies for a while but they serve up brilliant food. It's like a five star restaurant there, with fish and chips at half time and Ben and Jerry's Ice Cream if you want it too. Since Man City's new owners arrived they've improved the menu a lot.

Everton do a great job too. They provide tasty grub and a great welcome with it. It makes up for all the grief I take from Evertonians on the way to the stadium!

Appetites satisfied, we then make our way to the press box. Portsmouth, I'm sad to say again, is the worst I've been to in the Premier League. The last time I went there, it was tiny and you had to climb over people to get in to your seat.

I remember Steve commentating at one game down there and he said: "John's bum is now on the head of the man in front of me", as I was clambering over a guy. I nearly fell on the lad because I was laughing so much.

THE PHONE-IN
The football phone-in at the end of a game has become an essential part of the matchday. Whether you love it or hate it, you can't ignore it and every game we are guaranteed to get fans ringing up to have their say.

Years ago there was 'Sharpy' (Graeme Sharp) and 'Snods' (Ian Snodin) with me on the phone-in and we'd bounce off each other, taking it in turns to answer the Liverpool and Everton callers. It was really good and we usually ended up with plenty of banter which made the show lively.

Now, though, I often have to conduct the phone-in on my own because we rarely play on the same day as Everton. On occasions, you can find yourself answering the same questions a lot. There is only so much you can talk about after some games but it's always interesting to hear fans' opinions and to have a chat with them about issues that they obviously feel very strongly about.

When it's freezing and you've lost is the worst time to do a phone-in, as you might guess. Not only are you feeling down after a defeat but you're hanging about a nearly empty stadium and it's depressing.

You have to be careful, too, because you get callers pretending to be Reds, but they're really Man United or Everton fans trying to wind me up.

I remember one guy tried to correct me about Voronin. He said he was a good player. I'd had enough that day and went in to a right rant about him.

Some people come on just to argue with you rather than discuss something. I've described a few callers as idiots. I've been tempted to swear at some of them too, but you just can't. Thankfully most are sensible callers and genuine supporters who want to get something off their chest.

As a pundit it often feels like the phone-in is running '24:7'. People in Liverpool love talking about football because it got everyone through bad times here in the '80s. When the docks closed and lots of jobs were lost, football provided some solace. That hasn't really changed. It's still a football-mad city. Every Monday morning, wherever you are in Liverpool, there will be fans buzzing about a great result or wanting to talk about how bad such and such a player was at the weekend.

Because people recognise my face, it means everywhere you go, people want to chat about the club and the latest game. When you're doing well or after a cup final win such as Istanbul that's fantastic. You never get tired of discussing games like that. When it's going wrong, such as throughout 2009/10, it can be a challenge coming up with different responses to the same issues that are driving people mad.

As well as working as a pundit on the radio, I write columns for the Liverpool Echo newspaper and The Kop Magazine, which is a great read. The way it usually works is that the lads at the Echo and the Kop will give me a call and ask me a few questions about what's happening at Liverpool. As you can imagine, there's always plenty to talk about, be it good or bad. Then they will write it up in the form of an article. I know I can trust the lads at the ECHO and Kop to do a good job but sometimes things can go wrong when you speak to a journalist that you don't know. You have to be careful.

At the end of each chapter I'll be giving you a few top eights (after my favourite shirt number). We'll start with some about the media...

MY NAME IN PRINT

1. *'A local youngster who shows great potential with his flair for attack.'* **South Liverpool FC official pen pics, August 1978**

2. *'On current form, John Aldridge must be one of the best strikers in the Northern Premier League.'* **South Liverpool match programme, April 1979**

3. *'Player of the Month'.* **Daily Mirror, April 1985.** *(The Mirror was owned by Robert Maxwell and I played for Oxford then)*

4. *'Ian Rush look-a-like John Aldridge will today sign for Liverpool in a near £1 million deal.'* **Daily Mirror, January 1987**

5. *'Two goal hero John Aldridge, who said he might never play again after the Hillsborough tragedy claimed the lives of 95* Liverpool fans, spoke of "the most wonderful game of my life".* **Daily Mirror, May 1989** *(after we had reached the FA Cup final by beating Nottingham Forest 3-1. *Tony Bland, the 96th Hillsborough victim, died in 1993)*

6. *'Aldo plays like a Liverpool player. Knows his role, inside out. Takes the ball, back to goal, lays it off and moves. Sounds simple, looks even simpler but the consistency of the achievement takes it way beyond the ordinary'.* **Irish national newspaper, 1992**

7. *'Millions of people heard Aldridge call the official a dickhead'.* **Daily Mirror, June 1994.** *(More about THAT incident later...)*

8. *'John Aldridge will be offered the job as Republic of Ireland manager in the next 72 hours after Mick McCarthy resigned. Aldridge is the Football Association of Ireland's outstanding candidate. Ray Houghton is likely to be made his assistant'.* **Daily Mirror, November, 2002.** *(The job I should have had – see chapter 11)*

MY EIGHT FAVOURITE PUNDITS/COMMENTATORS
1. Alan Hansen (talks sense)
2. Ian Botham (does a great job on the cricket)
3. Brian Moore
4. Kenneth Wolstenholme
5. Alan Parry – a Garston lad, like me
6. Gerald Sinstadt – for the St Etienne game more than anything
7. Steve Hothersall
(I really enjoy working with Steve on Radio City, apart from the fact he always leaves too early to go to the game. Wigan is only 25 miles from my house but Steve leaves for it three hours before kick-off. It's a nightmare. He drives so slowly a milkfloat once overtook us on the motorway)
8. Daniel Mann
(I also worked with Dan at City before he moved on. He's a good commentator but one of the tightest people I've ever met in life, not just football)

MOST DIFFICULT GROUNDS TO GET TO
(The most difficult to get to first)
1. Selhurst Park
2. Upton Park
3. The Valley
4. Stamford Bridge
5. White Hart Lane
6. The Emirates
7. Craven Cottage
8. Fratton Park

PRESS ROOM GRUB
(In case you've ever wondered what the press get to eat at the match...)
1. Portsmouth – nice people but I didn't enjoy the food at times
2. Arsenal – five star food and dessert
3. Man City – curries, roast dinners and a few other choices
4. Liverpool – they do a lovely roast dinner

5. *Everton – really good breakfast for early derby kick-offs*
6. *Wigan – great pies, if you get there in time*
7. *Hull City – we had a brilliant curry on the last day of 2009/10*
8. *Blackburn – Thankfully Lancashire Hotpot has been on the menu for some years because it's usually the middle of winter when we go to Ewood*

MY VIEWS IN PRINT

It is disgusting... it is a man's game
'I would rather by punched than spat at. It is disgusting and there should be no place for it in football. It is a man's game'.
Liverpool Echo, March 2003. *(After El Hadji Diouf spitting incident at Celtic)*

Zidane has had his day... Steve has taken over
'If you take Ronaldhino out of the equation, then there aren't many players who come into consideration for being the best in the world... As far as midfield players are concerned then Zidane has had his day and so has Figo. They were both world class players but Steve has taken over their mantle for me'.
Kop Magazine, May 2006. *(After the 'Gerrard final' against West Ham)*

No light at the end of the tunnel
'It is difficult to remember a time in all my years following Liverpool that I have felt more deflated than now. Just look at the club. Negativity everywhere, no light at the end of the tunnel under an ownership that is beyond a joke. Nobody knows when or if the club will be sold, nobody knows which players are staying or going and the financial figures make for horrific reading. It's the worst possible scenario that you could ever have to face up to... how do we get out of the mess?'
Liverpool Echo, May 2010

I was 17 and standing on the Kop again

'I've been there for all the big nights, Bruges, St Etienne, all of them and this is up there again. When everyone in the stadium sings together like that, it is incredible. I was doing my commentary for Radio City but couldn't contain myself. I lost the plot again – big time. I was engrossed by it all. When we scored the goal, hit the bar, had one disallowed and then had penalties, it was like I was 17 and standing on the Kop again'. **Kop Magazine, May 2007** (after the Chelsea Champions League semi-final second leg at Anfield)

It shows that the players care

'One of the main qualities that you always want to see in a Liverpool player is passion. Which is why I was delighted to see the way Jamie Carragher responded to some slackness in the Liverpool defence at West Brom last weekend. For me, it shows that the players care'. **Liverpool Echo, May 2009** (after Jamie Carragher berated Alvaro Arbeloa during a game)

A toy factory for the world's richest men

'What a week with the megabucks takeover of Manchester City by Abu Dhabi. It's left me shaking my head and while City fans are on cloud nine, I've concluded that English football is now just a toy factory for the world's richest men. The game's changing and it is no longer what it was in so many ways. This great game of ours must remain connected properly with the supporters'. Liverpool Echo.co.uk, September 2008

The win laid a bit of a ghost for me

'Personally, I've been waiting for that kind of victory against Arsenal ever since 1989. There was the FA Cup final of 2001, but this was the biggest game between the teams since they won the league title against us at Anfield. The win certainly laid to rest a bit of a ghost for me'. **Liverpool Echo, April 2008** (after the 4-2 Champions League quarter final success over Arsenal at Anfield)

CHAPTER 2: GOALS

GET IN!

'A year or so ago I was on holiday in San Sebastian, the northern Spanish town where Aldo spent two seasons playing for Real Sociedad, prior to his move to Tranmere. On a few nights we got talking football in broken English with the locals. It was always the same when we asked them about Aldo.

"Ah, yes" they'd say, "Aldridge... goals!"

'The two words connect in any language'

— *Nick Hilton,
Liverpool Daily Post*

Cuttings I've kept from over the
years – including one where
Diego Maradona even has a few
words of praise for me...

GOALS ARE MY FORTUNE

When I was a baby, my mother went to see a fortune teller who told me I'd be gifted with my feet. She was probably just guessing but scoring 476 goals in my career shows the prediction was correct. It put me in the top 10 of all-time English goalscorers.

I know all of my 476 goals didn't come in the top flight. They were in different divisions, plus a few in Spain and some for Ireland. But that total puts me top of the list of all time post-war goalscorers in British football. I finished just ahead of Jimmy Greaves, one of the best strikers I've ever seen. To score so many at the top level was incredible and he got plenty of praise for it, unlike me.

Just how much my efforts go unnoticed was illustrated to me perfectly in 2003. Manchester United's Ruud Van Nistelrooy scored in 10 consecutive league games that year and the Dutch striker had everyone rightly talking about just how good he was and how well he'd done. What those people seemed to forget was I'd done the same thing during my time with Liverpool. I started my run in the last league game of 1986/87, in a 3-3 draw at Chelsea. I continued by scoring against Arsenal, Coventry City, West Ham, Oxford United, Charlton, Newcastle, Derby County, Portsmouth and QPR in the first nine league outings of 1987/88. It was ten league games in a row, just like Van Nistelrooy.

That run eventually helped me end the season with 26 goals, enough to claim the First Division Golden Boot. Yet again it is something that's rarely mentioned. I won a lot of honours in my career, including the League and FA Cup, but the award for top scorer meant so much to me.

It was so special because I'd done it for the club I loved, at the ground I loved. If I had achieved it with another side I would have been pleased, but it would not have been as good. By picking that up you are setting standards. Winning top-scorer proves you are one of the best in the country.

In Spain my ratio was also very good. In total I finished up with 40 goals in 75 league and cup appearances for the Basque side, a record that makes me proud. I also managed to set a club record for Sociedad by scoring in six consecutive league games. Nobody had ever done that. Sociedad weren't a big club either; in fact for one of the seasons we struggled a lot. Other players from English football went abroad and did nowhere near as well. Again though I didn't get much credit. If I'd have played for England, or been from London, I'd probably have got more exposure and recognition for what I did on the pitch.

WHY I WORE NUMBER EIGHT

From an early age I knew I was a goalscorer, but I wasn't sure how far that would take me in the game. All top strikers say goalscoring comes naturally and for me it was the same. I was just able to find space in the box and had the knack of putting the ball in the net. It was never something I really had to think about, I was just born with it. I used to score five and six goals in games for the school, eight was the most I managed in one match. Headers always gave me lots of satisfaction but I didn't care how I did it, as long as the ball went in. A tap-in was just as good as a spectacular volley.

I never scored many from long range, the few I did get I can still recall with the best being in a pre-season friendly for Tranmere against Falkirk. It came from the halfway line after the Scottish team had just scored.

We were getting ready to restart the game and I told my fellow striker Gary Bennett to just roll the ball to me. "Why?" he asked. "Just do it," I said.

The keeper was standing on the edge of the 18-yard box and I smashed it over his head right into the top corner. I later found out he was on trial from Rangers. I'm sure that didn't help his cause when it came to getting a permanent move. Just before the game began again I turned to look at the TV gantry and noticed there were no cameras there to film the action. I was absolutely gutted. Not many players score goals like that, I certainly didn't, and it would have been nice to have a recording of it.

With me being a striker it was only natural and inevitable that a Liverpool player in the same position would become my favourite. It was Roger Hunt; I simply loved him. His record was unbelievable too, 286 goals in 492 appearances is brilliant. Sadly it's rarely talked about now. He did amazing things for Liverpool and was one of the club's best ever players. He was a World Cup winner too, yet people don't seem to even realise that. He was the quiet man of the 1966 national side. The likes of Geoff Hurst, Alan Ball and Bobby Moore seemed to get all the attention. Some think Hunt didn't even play in the final.

I eventually met Roger and couldn't speak highly enough of him. He was the reason why I wanted to wear number eight. People suggested I didn't want to wear nine at Liverpool because it had been Rushie's number and I wouldn't be able to handle the pressure that came with it. That was rubbish. I wore eight at Oxford and Newport when I could, and ten now and again. But I always wanted to be number eight because of Hunt.

He was my idol, even if someone else scored my favourite ever goal for the Reds. There are hundreds to choose from when I'm asked this question. But Tommy Smith's bullet header in the 1977 European Cup final is probably my favourite. Borussia Monchengladbach had got it back to 1-1 through Allan Simonsen and the situation looked bad for us.

The Germans were starting to dominate when Tommy intervened. Making it 2-1 at that time gave us the belief to go on and win our first European Cup. It was supposed to be Tommy's last game before he retired so we all thought he'd finished in the perfect fashion. Instead he changed his mind and carried on for one more year before leaving to join Swansea City.

IT TAKES TWO

I developed an understanding with all of my striking partners, although some of the partnerships flourished more than others. I always had most trouble predicting what Tony Cascarino was going to do. 'Cas' was a great lad and a hard worker who would run through a brick wall for you. The problem was we didn't always know what he was going to do with his second touch. It might have been a pass or a shot but we were never sure. It was hard to anticipate what he was going to do.

Others who I had a lot more success with included Peter Beardsley, Niall Quinn and Ian Rush. At Oxford I worked alongside Billy Whitehurst. He was a fearsome character who Alan Hansen admitted to being frightened of. In fact, I think he said he was the hardest player of all time. I wasn't surprised to hear that. Billy was really strong and without fear, even managers were afraid to disagree with him and wouldn't dare try to substitute him.

There's one funny story I remember about Billy when he first joined Oxford. I think he signed on a Thursday, he had his first training session on Friday and then his first game was against Liverpool at Anfield the day later. He was sitting in the visitors' changing room on the day of the match and the manager Maurice Evans started to read out the team. Billy stands up and says: "Excuse me, boss, can I just say something?"

He says: "I had a dream last night and we played these Scousers, and we beat them 2-1". We were all wondering what he was on about. The game started and Oxford were getting beaten 2-0 when Billy gets a chance to score. He goes up for a header by the penalty spot, right in front of the goal but misses.

When he lands back on the ground, he jars his back. It's really sore but because he's at Anfield, he plays on for the last 15 minutes of the half. I tell him to go off because he's in pain and running like Max Wall but he won't.

At half-time, he realises he can't carry on and he goes off. We end up losing 4-0 and we all sit down sheepishly in the changing room. We put our heads down as the manager comes in and prepare ourselves for a dressing down. Liverpool played very well but we were poor.

Maurice Evans comes in and says: "Right boys", but before he can begin, Billy stands up again and says: "Sorry lads, I've got to say... that dream I had last night... it wasn't a dream, it was a bloody nightmare!"

If any centre-back ever attempted to rough me up Billy usually had a word and their attitude altered instantly. We worked well together, but not as well as the man he had replaced at Oxford, another Billy by the name of Hamilton.

He had appeared for Northern Ireland at the 1982 World Cup and was my ideal strike partner. We simply clicked on the pitch and during the 1984/85 season we registered 51 goals between us in all competitions, enough to ensure Oxford were promoted to the top division as champions.

Later on in my career at Tranmere I played up front on my own, because with the players we had, a 4-5-1 formation suited us best. I didn't mind being the lone striker if the midfield players supported me well, and the lads did that. During my first season in La Liga it was different. I was usually isolated and frustrated up front, particularly during our away games. Thankfully that changed when Dalian Atkinson arrived from Sheffield Wednesday.

I was delighted he came to the club because he helped me on the field and was brilliant company off it. I'd never met Dalian before then but he was a great fella and, although I've lost touch with him now and must do something about it, we became close friends. I knew how tough it was trying to settle in a new country so I tried to ease the process.

On a Monday or Thursday night, depending on whether we had a midweek game or not, Dalian would phone my house. I'd tell Joan that I couldn't be bothered going out and ask her to answer on my behalf.

When she put the phone down she would start giving me grief, saying Dalian was alone and I should go for a beer to keep him company. Eventually I'd agree and meet him for a few drinks and a laugh. I'd have a couple of beers and he'd be sipping Jack Daniels and Coke. Joan never knew Dalian and I had organised the whole thing earlier that day.

Everything with him was a big laugh, even football. He never took it seriously. There was no doubt he had real talent, as he proved for a time with Aston Villa when they nearly won the Premier League under Ron Atkinson in 1992/93. But he'll probably admit himself he wasn't serious enough about it to consistently play at his best.

PLAYING WITH STEVIE... AND MARADONA

We did work very well together in Spain, with the highlight probably being the night we won 3-1 in the Nou Camp against the newly crowned champions. Dalian created two goals for me and I set up one for him. We also both got on the scoresheet in a 3-2 win at Real Madrid. Our styles complemented each other very well.

When I look at football now I think another player I'd combine well with would be Steven Gerrard. I was an out and out goalscorer and needed someone with me who was more creative. Stevie would be that man; he'd be my perfect partner up front. I'd love to have played alongside him. He would have got his 20 plus goals, and I would have got my 30, or maybe even more. I think it would have worked very well because of the number of assists he would have provided.

Another dream strike partner would have been a certain Argentinian number 10. Tranmere played against Ascoli in the Anglo-Italian Cup in 1994 and afterwards their manager, Alberto Bigon, came over to me and said: "Aldridge, well played. I wanted to sign you. I tried to get you when I was at Napoli. I wanted you and Maradona up front." I nearly collapsed when I heard that. I don't know if there was any truth in it but even now I still imagine the prospect, wow. I would have scored around 80 goals every season if I'd played with him.

I've kept a newspaper cutting, which you can see at the start of this chapter. It's from 1992 and Maradona is praising Ireland after we played Spain in Seville and drew 0-0 in a World Cup qualifier.

I scored but it was ruled out and Maradona, who was still the world's most famous player at that time, said: "The goal he scored was as big as a house. I don't understand why it was disallowed, there was no offside in my opinion.

"I think it's a pity he's not playing First Division football. He proved that he still has a lot to offer".

I've never heard one of my goals described like that but nevertheless it's great to have someone like him say nice things about you.

PAYING THE PENALTY FOR THAT MISS

...It's me against Dave Beasant. From 12 yards I strike the ball past him once, twice, three times and again. And once more to make it five successful penalties out of five attempts. The former Wimbledon keeper doesn't save any of my efforts...

Unfortunately, that was a penalty shootout for charity a few years ago. When it was the real thing back in 1988 we all know what happened.

People don't remember that I scored nearly 500 goals. What they do always recall without fail is the fact I missed that spot-kick against Wimbledon in the '88 FA Cup final.

Over two decades later, somebody still mentions it to me almost every week. As everyone knows we lost the game 1-0 and with it the chance to win the Double – it would have been Liverpool's second in the space of three years. Even as I sank to my knees on the Wembley turf that day I still couldn't believe Dave had saved my spot-kick.

I felt terrible. Within seconds I'd been substituted too. Kenny had planned to take me off even before then. I drank a lot of beer that night to try to forget all about it.

Alan Hansen's testimonial was due to take place the following Monday. He was furious and told me that I'd cost him thousands of pounds because if we'd won both trophies more people would have turned up for his game. I also missed a penalty in a practice match for Ireland a few weeks later. Ray Houghton and Ronnie Whelan were winding me up for ages about it.

The Wembley miss did affect me for a while that summer. I'd be lying if I said it didn't. Thankfully the European Championships took my mind off it. Then I scored twice in the Charity Shield in August, also against Wimbledon.

That helped me overcome what had gone on. It was still a while before I took another penalty though. I let Jan do it instead, even in a big game against Man United at Anfield. Eventually I reclaimed the responsibility when he was injured.

A lot of people use the fact that I scored so many penalties as a reason to detract from my record. I completely disagree with that. You need balls to stand up and handle the responsibility. As I know too well, it's not easy and missing isn't nice. It earned me an unwanted place in the history books.

A major part of the challenge is also overcoming attempts by opponents to put you off. Plenty of players did exactly that by mouthing various words or obscenities at me. Dennis Wise and his pals were particularly loud in '88. He also did the same a few years later when we'd both moved on and Tranmere were facing Chelsea in the Rumbelows Cup. I don't think his efforts affected me either way, the first time I missed and the second time I scored. Dennis wasn't the only one to try it.

My way of dealing with it was to grab the ball and do keepy-ups or just turn my back. I'd let whoever was involved just chat away to the ref.

THE ALDO SHUFFLE

Having the confidence required wasn't the main reason why I took pens. It was simply because I was greedy. I wanted to score goals all the time; by any means necessary. Famously I developed a great technique that led to me scoring a lot of pens. It also brought me a lot of criticism. 'The Aldo shuffle', as it was christened, was a form of cheating according to some people in the game, such as TV pundit Jimmy Greaves.

The idea originally came into my head after I scored a goal past Gerry Peyton of Fulham. I dummied a shot from close range and he dived to one side, leaving me with an open goal. Gerry was a friend of mine through the Ireland squad and said he hated me for doing that to him. We used to call him 'The Haymaker' because if you got in the way of one of his punches you'd be knocked out. Thankfully he was only joking about wanting to get me after I'd scored.

Following the game I thought if I could dummy the ball like that and make a keeper move before a penalty was struck it would be easy to score. I worked on it in training at Oxford and eventually perfected it. I've seen plenty of top strikers in the world doing it over the years and it makes me proud when they score.

You needed a lot of composure to do it well. Now and again you might be trying to put it right in the far corner and miss the target or hit the post. But most of the time it was successful. There was also the odd occasion when clever keepers just stood up and didn't move. Then you had to just smash the ball.

It doesn't matter what your technique is, practicing is always the best way to become a good penalty taker.

With Ireland we did loads of it because Niall (Quinn) would always go in goal for shootouts after training. He's a decent keeper, as he proved when Tony Coton was sent off during a Man City versus Derby County game in 1990/91. Niall took his place and saved Dean Saunders' penalty. We had to get three out of three to win £10 from him. If you missed one, he took the money. We practiced so often I think that helped us against Romania at the 1990 World Cup. All the lads scored to help us go through to the quarter-finals.

Steven Gerrard is another great example of how hours on the training ground helps you improve your chances of converting from the spot.

At times he looks like he'll never miss. That wasn't always the case. He's obviously worked hard at it and rarely fails to score. He looks very confident whenever he puts the ball on the spot. That is another huge part of it.

When a shootout comes along you have to be full of confidence, almost arrogance. When Liverpool won in Istanbul I thought all the players looked full of belief as they placed the ball.

I never thought Didi Hamann would miss. Even though they weren't the best players Djibril Cisse and Vladimir Smicer also looked really confident. John Arne Riise missed, but that was a great save from Dida.

So I think being arrogant about it definitely improves your chances of finding the net.

WINDMILLS, CIGARS AND GETTING SHIRTY
Finally I'd done it.

I ran straight to the Irish fans to mark my first goal for my country. They were initially going mad too. Then they suddenly stopped celebrating.

I turned around to see an offside flag raised. Ronnie Whelan was laughing his head off and roaring at me to get back on the pitch, as Luxembourg were taking the free-kick. I'd been waiting for that moment for a long time and wanted to celebrate it in style. Instead I felt like a right prick.

That was also how I ended up looking after a UEFA Cup goal for Sociedad too. I was delighted and swung my arms around and around, like a windmill. I have to be honest and say it didn't work. I just looked pathetic.

From those experiences I learned that my best method for

celebration was to always keep it simple.

Celebrations are part of football and shouldn't lead to yellow cards. A referee has never scored a goal so they can't understand how a player feels when it happens. If they did, they wouldn't hand out a booking for taking your shirt off. That doesn't really cause any harm. It's only if someone is trying to cause trouble with their celebration that they should be disciplined.

Even those who only have good intentions can still experience problems in the aftermath of a goal going in. I found that out during Tranmere's aforementioned 3-1 victory against Chelsea in the Rumbelows Cup in 1991.

After scoring I made a cigar gesture to their fans to indicate we were in control of the tie and going through.

Their goalkeeper, Kevin Hitchcock, thought I was aiming it at him. At the end of the match he came running after me and shouted: "Don't you be giving me the cigar."

A brawl nearly broke out. I got to know Kev years later and we had a good laugh about it.

There are some great celebrations in the game now that thankfully don't cause too many problems, with players doing backflips, somersaults and tumbles.

If I was able to do any of those I would have. I could have pulled a mask from my sock, as others have done, or kissed a camera like Steven Gerrard did at Old Trafford. I just never thought of it. Those moments really make me laugh. They're entertaining and what fans want to see.

It's not something which we ever want to witness again but I thought Eric Cantona's Kung Fu kick on a supporter at Crystal Palace in 1995 was priceless.

It rightly caused outrage. I could understand why people disapproved, but I also felt it would have been a great way to celebrate a goal.

Scoring and then doing that to someone who had been giving you loads of abuse would have been the perfect response.

EIGHT STRIKE PARTNERS I PLAYED WITH

1. Niall Quinn (brilliant in the air and on the floor. I read him well)

2. Ian Rush (people said we couldn't play together. We totally disagreed)

3. Peter Beardsley (he didn't make many goals directly for me but his movement led to plenty)

4. Billy Hamilton (we were a perfect combination. For whatever reason we worked together better than anyone else who I played with)

5. Dalian Atkinson (so much potential, great to play alongside)

6. Tony Cascarino (his second touch was a header. No. I'm only joking! He was a good foil for me)

7. Chris Malkin (we did well together, he always used his pace to create space)

8. Billy Whitehurst (nobody ever messed with him and I could see why. He scared defenders)

EIGHT STADIUMS I PLAYED IN...

1. Nou Camp (six goals in three games there)

2. Lansdowne Road (the scene of some great days and nights)

3. The Bernabeu

4. Estadio Atocha (loved it, very close to the pitch and similar to West Ham before it was re-developed)

5. Anfield (home).

6. Somerton Park (Newport County – very open and gave me a great insight into professional football)

7. The Manor Ground (very similar to Atocha, an intimidating place for away teams)

8. Giants Stadium, New Jersey (USA '94)

...AND TWO I DIDN'T PLAY IN BUT WISH I HAD

Croke Park. It's a unique place, one of the best grounds I've ever been to. And the new Lansdowne, Aviva Stadium, as it is now called. It looks like a phenomenal new stadium.

TOP EIGHT FAVOURITE LIVERPOOL STRIKERS*

1. Roger Hunt
2. Kenny Dalglish
3. Ian Rush
4. Robbie Fowler
5. Kevin Keegan
6. Fernando Torres
7. Ian St John
8. John Toshack

(* Michael Owen was brilliant for us and I loved him, but he really hurt me when he went to Manchester United).

MY EIGHT FAVOURITE CELEBRATIONS

1. Robbie Fowler sniffing the line (he was giving back some stick to those who dished it out).
2. Steven Gerrard kissing the camera (Old Trafford)
3. Robbie Keane's cartwheel (I like the fact he's kept doing it over the years)
4. Michael Owen's hand-rubbing (as seen at Newcastle)
5. Any time a player puts on a mask
6. Lee Sharpe's corner flag routine
7. Referee Mike Reed's celebration after Liverpool scored against Leeds in 2000 (Reed later claimed he was congratulating himself on his decision to play an advantage, which led to the goal...)
8. Hands in the air (simple)

CHAPTER 3: FRIENDS AND FOES

RIVALS

1. **Manchester United**
2. **Everton**
3. **Leeds United**
4. **Arsenal**
5. **Borussia Monchengladbach**
6. **Nottingham Forest**
7. **Bruges**
8. **Chelsea**

Liverpool's biggest rivals
in my time as a Kopite...

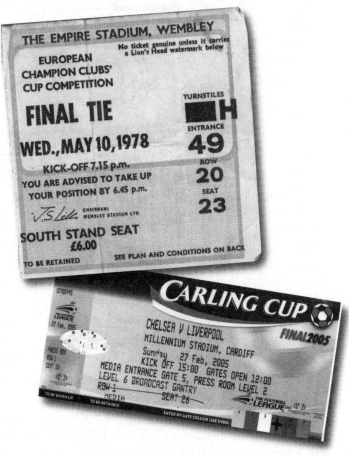

Two rivals and two different outcomes. I went to see us beat Bruges at Wembley for the 1978 European Cup final and was working for the media when Chelsea got the better of us in the Carling Cup in 2005...

UNITED...

IF you ask any Liverpool fan who they would like to be guaranteed a victory against the answer would be instant; Manchester United is the club we all want to beat each year. Winning 4-1 at their place in March 2009 was one of the sweetest days to be a Red in recent seasons.

Once the rivalry between the two teams used to be fairly amicable. Matt Busby was Liverpool skipper before he went to Old Trafford and of course went on to establish himself as a legendary manager, winning the European Cup in 1968. Back then the clubs got on.

Now they rarely seem to see eye to eye, with our former boss Rafa and Fergie clearly disliking each other. Rafa came out with his now infamous list of 'facts' during a press conference in January, 2009 and the two managers even came close to squaring up during one game.

On the terraces that relationship used to be even worse at times and I got a taste of it when I was a young Liverpool fan. There was always a lot of fighting around football grounds back in the 1970s. It was part of the culture and you always knew there could be a chance of ending up on the receiving end, especially away from home.

On this occasion, I had gone to Manchester on the special football train after work. I remember it well. I'm not sure what sparked it but something happened outside Old Trafford and the next thing I knew I was surrounded by about 40 of their fans. It was a very scary experience.

I was just 17 at the time and I ended up getting kicked from pillar to post before the United fans tried to throw me in front of a bus. The driver just braked in time before he reached me and opened the doors. I quickly jumped in and escaped from them, getting off at the next stop further down the road.

I still went into the game but I made sure I left Old Trafford that day just before the end because I didn't want to be caught up in it all again. The match wasn't the best and finished 0-0 anyway.

But my early dart didn't work as when we got outside the Mancs were waiting for us. There was about five or six of us and a load of them but thankfully the police were there and helped out.

They walked with us down the Matt Busby Way. The United fans were still watching and slowly following at a distance waiting for their chance. When we got to a set of traffic lights further down the road, the cops said: "Now run for your lives!"

We did, and about 50 of their supporters chased us, even over nearby railway lines. Our group got separated and, as I was on my own, I jumped in a taxi to the train station. I didn't like Manchester United before then, and I certainly didn't after that.

Unfortunately at the 2003 Worthington Cup final between the teams at the Millennium Stadium, I had confirmation that some things haven't changed.

I was doing co-commentary on the radio when I noticed a Liverpool fan, only about 15-years-old, getting battered by some United supporters. This was inside the ground, not outside. The lad was on the wrong side of the divide between the two sets of fans and he paid for that by getting kicked around. Those dishing out the beating weren't youngsters either; they were men in their thirties and forties.

The bad feeling between us and them isn't all one way. It's got to the stage where both sets of fans are as bad as each other, although it has to be said that it's just a small minority who might still go looking for trouble and things aren't anything like as bad as they used to be a few decades ago.

18 TITLES EACH IS HARD TO TAKE

Apart from taking a kicking outside their ground, one of the other reasons I had a dislike for the Red Devils when I was growing up was simply because they had some really good teams and were a big danger to Liverpool. They were our rivals because they had great players like Bobby Charlton,

Denis Law and George Best. We had Roger Hunt, Ian St John and Peter Thompson and obviously you wanted to beat them and finish ahead of them in the league table.

That wasn't a problem when I was growing up because Liverpool were clearly the better team back then. I think the rivalry between fans was more about which club was bigger. The Merseyside derby was more important in those days because Everton were more of a threat to us in football terms. As a kid, my stomach would churn when we were going into games against the Blues because you knew it was big – now that applies when you face United. They've caught up with us in league titles and they've overtaken us in terms of money, transfer fees and wages they can afford to pay and the stadium. It is very hard to take.

BEHIND ENEMY LINES

I got some revenge for what those United fans did to me by netting the first goal of Alex Ferguson's reign. It came in November, 1986, when Oxford won 2-0 at the Manor Ground and I opened the scoring with a penalty. When I moved on from Oxford, as it happened I didn't do that well against United. During my time as a player at Anfield we drew two – including an amazing 3-3 at Anfield – and won one of the four games I was involved in.

Old Trafford might be the home of our enemy but the biggest game of my life also took place there; the replay of the semi-final that had been abandoned after the Hillsborough Disaster. We had to win that game against Nottingham Forest for the fans who had tragically passed away in Sheffield, and their families. I was very proud to score twice.

Now I go to Old Trafford whenever Liverpool visit there. To get to the press entrance you have to walk from the car park through quite a few fans and you sometimes get a few people shouting abuse on the way in and out, especially if we've won. But it's never too bad. I've obviously met the right people. A lot of Irish go to Old Trafford so maybe that's why I don't get as much stick as others with Liverpool connections. I know some of my former team-mates, and others, get plenty.

THE DIFFERENCE BETWEEN NEVILLE AND ROONEY

One such trip was in January 2006. Liverpool played really well and definitely didn't deserve to lose that Sunday afternoon. To do so thanks to a last minute Rio Ferdinand header was really sickening. Then having Gary Neville taunt the away section made it even more difficult to take.

I can put myself in Neville's shoes; if we'd scored a late winner against United when I was playing I might have gone mad celebrating too. Although I'd like to think I'd have shown more tact than the full-back. I certainly wouldn't have run 60 yards to goad the fans like he did. I thought that was a naive thing to do for an experienced professional.

That moment wasn't the reason why I dislike him though; it's because of how disrespectful he's been to the people of Merseyside. "I can't stand Liverpool, I can't stand Liverpool people, I can't stand anything to do with them," he once said. Because of comments like that, Scousers understandably despise him in return. The other things he does just reinforce their dislike of him.

My feelings for Neville are the complete opposite to how I look upon Wayne Rooney. To cross the divide between the cities and play for one of the other teams as Wayne has done would be difficult for anyone, to do it as a kid takes even more courage.

When he was only about 15 or 16 I met Wayne and his dad at the races. I told him he was already good enough and that his age didn't matter. He could do it in the Premier League so had nothing to worry about. That's proved to be correct as he's gone on to become one of the best players in the world. In recent years he's also matured a lot, which everyone does as they grow up. Huge amounts of Liverpudlians, both red and blue, absolutely hate him. But I simply can't, I think he is brilliant. We should be proud of the fact that one of the best talents around comes from our city. If he had moved to Arsenal or abroad it wouldn't have been such a problem. It's the fact he went to United which has led to such a bad reaction and that's a shame.

KNOCKING THEM OFF THEIR PERCH

Rooney's presence at the other end of the East Lancs gives the rivalry another twist. United sing about hating Scousers, but then chant his name in the next sentence. Meanwhile, a brilliant Scouser who should be the pride of the city is hated by both Liverpool and Everton. Only in football could that happen!

The rivalry and banter can be very nasty and spiteful. They were very jealous when we were the dominant team in England. Now there is a lot of envy from our side because of what Alex Ferguson has achieved. Since he had that row with Kenny after the 3-3 draw in '88, Fergie has always had something against us. He famously said he wanted to knock the club 'off its fucking perch' and he's done it – although we're still by far the most successful British team in Europe. Being the best used to go in cycles. But now that also depends a bit more on the money element. Until Liverpool set some firm foundations behind the scenes, we are going to find it very difficult to even catch up, never mind overtake United. That's a sad fact.

EVERTON...

I can be in a shop waiting to get served and know the person behind the counter is an Evertonian. Sometimes Blues just don't react too well when they see me. The same applies when I'm in my car. People will look at me and then refuse to let me out at a busy junction. As they drive away I'll see an Everton sticker on the back window. It makes me laugh and I don't take too much notice of it but they shouldn't treat me differently. I'm from the same city and I'm the same as them; I love my club too. There is nothing wrong with that.

There are plenty of Evertonians in my family; I've got cousins and nephews who are Blues. That's the way it is in Liverpool. A lot of it comes from your family, my dad was a Red and that's what influenced me. I loved playing football at the back of my house when I was really young; that was how I started. I wasn't a Liverpool or Everton fan then. I was just into the game. Then my dad took me to watch Liverpool and I started supporting them.

In school, everyone I knew was interested in the game. That was the problem when the derby came around. We were all desperate for our team to win. The thought of losing and coming in on Monday morning was something none of us relished. The Evertonians would rip you to shreds with their remarks, if they'd won. After some defeats I often thought about staying off school for a few days. But if you did that you'd get even more grief when you did show up. The Evertonian lads would be waiting for you, building up a great list of jibes. So if we won, it was more of a relief, than anything else.

One of my first ever 'away' games was actually a short trip to Goodison Park in December, 1973. I was in the Park End and saw Alan Waddle score his only goal for us as we won 1-0 in a typically close encounter. Later on I got to play with him at Newport County. I remember it well because I had to do all the running up front, Alan definitely wasn't a workaholic is a kind way of putting it!

MY PART IN THE '86 DOUBLE

During 1982/83 Newport were drawn against Everton in both the League Cup and the FA Cup. Facing them always gave me extra motivation. When it came to the FA Cup meeting I wasn't 100 per cent right but managed to pass a fitness test. We drew 1-1 at Somerton Park; Kevin Sheedy got a very fortunate last minute equaliser for them. When we went to Goodison Park for the replay I scored a bicycle kick but we ended up losing 2-1.

At Oxford we had some good battles with Everton too, particularly the game in 1985/86 at the Manor Ground. They were going for the title and we needed a win to help us escape relegation. We beat them 1-0 in a midweek fixture. My mate Les Phillips scored the goal and on the same night Liverpool won at Leicester to take back control of the championship. We had a great celebration afterwards because I'd helped Liverpool. The following weekend they won the league at Stamford Bridge, so I felt like I'd played a small part in their success.

A week and a half on from that day I seriously considered travelling to Wembley for the first all-Merseyside FA Cup Final. Instead I ended up having a few cans in my house watching it on TV, and really enjoyed the second half as we came from behind to claim the Double.

HIGHS AND LOWS

I only played in the derby six times and we usually did pretty well in those games, only suffering one defeat. Even when they ended our long unbeaten league record in '88 I wasn't on the pitch. I was out injured at the time and went along to Goodison to watch the lads. I sat in the players' lounge where the staff kindly left on the TV for me to watch the action and provided me with free ale. I enjoyed myself, even if it wasn't a great day for the team.

Despite our usually good record against our neighbours I never felt I did well on a personal level. Because the games meant so much to me I was too wound up and couldn't perform at my best. I actually hated playing in them. You could never enjoy it, everything was so frantic. The ball was like a hot potato that you really had to fight to get hold of and keep. It was only when you were 2-0 up that you could relax, enjoy it and think about having a pint afterwards.

The last two times I came up against Everton as a Liverpool player were both in May '89. They were very different days for me.

The first meeting was in the league at Goodison, our return to action after the Hillsborough Disaster. It finished 0-0 and I got replaced by Rushie with around 20 minutes left. I was really pissed off because I thought it meant Kenny was going to leave me on the bench for the FA Cup semi-final the following weekend. So I went and took out my frustrations in the dressing room. I lost the plot completely and started trashing the place. I think it was a combination of frustration and my grief coming out after all that had gone on. I'd been to so many funerals I think it took its toll.

Later that same month our FA Cup final was against the Blues and I scored after just four minutes. It was my first touch because Everton had kicked off and we hadn't really had possession. My last touch a year earlier had been the penalty miss. Kenny had brought me off straight away after Dave Beasant had made the save in 1988. 12 months on I was almost in the same spot in front of the same goal. I hit the shot early and I think that caught out Neville Southall because he didn't expect it. I'd already made my mind up as the ball was coming to me. The perfectly weighted pass from Steve McMahon meant I didn't need to take a touch. I knew I was going to try and bend it in to the corner. Thankfully that's where it finished. I felt really sorry for Everton that day because everybody wanted Liverpool to win after what had happened. It wasn't an easy situation for them. Their fans, team and manager were magnificent about it all, they were really dignified.

I WOULD HAVE SIGNED FOR EVERTON
Even though pulling on a Liverpool shirt was a dream come true for me, I would definitely have joined Everton if the time was right and they had made a firm offer for me. Early on in my career, Howard Kendall was watching Glenn Cockerill in a

game where I scored the only goal.

After that I heard he was interested in me but for whatever reason nothing materialised. When it was obvious I was coming back from Spain to England in 1991 Howard was interested again and was in his second spell in charge at Everton. I've spoken to him about it since and he said he thought it wouldn't be fair to bring me to Goodison as I was such a well-known Liverpool fan. He felt the attention I would have received could have made my life difficult. But I was a professional and I would have had no problem with it.

BITTER BLUES?

Of all the former players I know, my fellow co-commentator at Radio City 'Snods' (Ian Snodin) is probably the bitterest! I don't know if bitter is the right word though... he can take it to extremes, although it's just because he feels strongly about his team, like I do.

I can understand how Blues feel in a way because we think of Manchester United in the same way as Everton do us. You get fed up with them winning all the time and taking the piss out of you. Everton have had that from us for years. It would annoy anybody so maybe they have a right to be upset, or bitter as we say.

When I was a player there was rivalry and banter between the two groups, but it was always good-natured. Now it's not always the case as I found out when Fernando Torres scored the only goal against Everton at Anfield in 2008.

I went for a few beers afterwards to celebrate but some Evertonians, guys in their 40s and 50s, started giving me grief as I walked into the pub. I tried to have a laugh with them and brush it off but they were having none of it. One of them shouted "murderer" straight in my face, referring of course to the tragic Heysel disaster of 1985. That was a very nasty comment and went beyond any rivalry. I was brought up with more respect for people than that. Some could laugh it off, I couldn't. So I asked him to step outside.

He refused and all of his mates started to gang up on me. There was around 10 or 15 of them, and a few Reds backing me up. I wisely decided I should leave. The last thing I wanted was Liverpudlians and Evertonians fighting in the pub. Every club has 'supporters' like that. Thankfully the vast majority of Everton fans I know don't behave in such a way.

A CITY TO BE PROUD OF

I think the logistics of the two teams sharing a new stadium would be difficult but you could do it. If the two clubs continue to have issues off the pitch in terms of owners or partners putting up the necessary funds then the shared stadium will have to be back on the agenda again. In those circumstances it would be very necessary for us, and probably our only choice.

But having said that, maybe the time to share has passed now. 10 or 15 years ago would probably have been the best time. For me it would only be worth doing now if it was a bigger and better stadium than anything else around, a bit like the new Wembley, impressive to look at and with a huge capacity. My main worry would be that if you did have a joint stadium each club would lose a little of its unique identity. Keeping that intact would be the problem.

The Milan clubs have managed to do it very well, and I think if there is another city that could do it then it would be Liverpool. In a way it could bring the fans together and help repair the relationship between both sides because it would be something to be very proud of.

Liverpool is a unique place and I think it's going to get even better. We're already seeing a lot more visitors coming to the city and with other new developments, there's no reason why that won't continue to be the case.

The 2008 Capital of Culture year was a great achievement, the new city centre and redesigned waterfront look fantastic, and having the joint stadium would be another reason for Scousers to feel very proud.

ENGLAND V IRELAND

"One of our caps is worth 20 appearances for Ireland," Steve McMahon would always tell me.

When I was at Liverpool we had a good collection of Irish and English players. I'd always chat with Steve, Barnesie and Peter Beardsley about what was going on with each country. We'd all take the piss out of each other. We had the last laugh because we beat them in Stuttgart in 1988 and they couldn't beat us at the World Cup or in the qualifiers for Euro '92. The games between the countries had a real derby feel because we knew each other so well. Our performances in those games really showed what we were capable of. And even in some of the draws we deserved more, the 1-1 at Wembley being the most obvious. It was probably one of Ireland's best ever displays, particularly away from home. Ray Houghton won't mind me saying he missed a sitter right at the end. I suppose he scored the winner in Stuttgart so we couldn't be too critical.

I think the England lads were envious of our set-up in many ways. When we went to Ireland we always had a good time, Jack let us have a few beers and we could just relax. They could never relax in the build up to games because of the pressure that came with playing for England. We'd sometimes go on international duty even if we were carrying an injury. They sometimes said they were looking to get injured so they wouldn't have to go away! It was an arduous time for the lads, and there were lots of splits in their camp, with different cliques from different clubs.

Our main motivation for winning against England came from the journalists, rather than the players we faced. When we first started to do well by reaching Euro '88 the English press picked up on the fact that some of us weren't first generation Irish and referred to us as 'mercenaries' – basically laughing at us. It was mainly the London based journalists. That did us a favour and we were always thankful to them because it made us even more determined. We knew going out onto that field there was no way England were ever going to beat us.

We had lads from Liverpool, London, Scotland and Wales, as well as Ireland of course. But we all played because we had affection for the country, no other reason.

I looked upon the chance to wear an Ireland shirt as a gift from my ancestors who came from Athlone. We knew we couldn't get at the journalists themselves, but the next best thing was doing well against their beloved team.

We rammed their taunts down their throats with our performances. Jack Charlton never needed any team talk for those fixtures.

DIVIDED LOYALTIES – IT'S JUST NOT CRICKET

I always support Ireland against England in everything, or almost everything.

The only time I wasn't sure about who to shout for was when they faced each other at the 2007 Cricket World Cup in the West Indies.

I'm a big cricket fan and played for the Liverpool Schoolboys team. When the countries played I decided I wanted England to win because the Irish team had no chance of going all the way in the competition, whereas the English side had. That was quite odd for me. It didn't feel 100 per cent right.

I'm so into cricket I even went to the Ashes at Old Trafford in 2005. A mate of mine from the Daily Mail had sorted the tickets for my son Paul and me.

All we had to do was pick them up at the ground. But when we arrived there was no sign of them. We were waiting around outside for ages when this guy, one of the stewards I think, said: "Just come in lads." Naturally we did.

We were standing against the wall having free drinks, with the Aussie team and all the WAGs sitting up above us. We'd been there for about two hours watching the game when another steward asked us to move. We just went to this nearby doorway, and one of us stood on either side.

Then Adam Gilchrist got caught in the slips and walked off the pitch, right through this door in between me and Paul.

"Unlucky mate" our Paul said.

He was being genuine and wasn't taking the piss. Gilchrist just gave him the worst set of daggers I've ever seen. I thought he was going to hit us with his bat.

TRANMERE V BOLTON

At times when I was at Tranmere, it felt like we were playing in a derby each week.

We had to be up for every game because we were usually in trouble at the bottom of the table, or underdogs in the cups. Every game mattered but Bolton eventually became the game we all looked towards more than any other. It's not stretching the truth to say that everybody from each club hated the other side, from fans to players to coaching staff.

The main reason for that was Sam Allardyce and his actions before the second leg of the 2000 Worthington Cup semi-final. It's fair to say I'm not a fan of his. Whenever we bump into each other now no more than 'hello' is said.

The first semi-final match at the Reebok had resulted in a narrow 1-0 victory for us after which Sam had criticised how we played. Despite coming to our place trailing, he was sure his team would be going to Wembley and told anyone who'd listen.

It was in nearly every paper I picked up and those I didn't have to hand I managed to get my hands on, such as the Bolton Evening News.

There were loads of quotes from him and their goalkeeper, Steve Banks, too. They said we'd been lucky in the first game and talked about how they were going to turn us over this time. I didn't like that attitude, it was very arrogant. It's an old trick but I pinned up all the cuttings in the dressing room to remind my players of what had been said.

We were 2-0 up in 20 minutes – 3-0 on aggregate – and it was a case of 'job done, thank you very much Sam' before we'd even reached half time.

By the final whistle, David Kelly had added another goal just for good measure. A nice bonus for me was the fact that I bought my villa in Portugal with the money I got from taking Tranmere to the final.

MAKING IT PAY

Athletic Bilbao were our local rivals when I played for Real Sociedad after leaving Liverpool in 1989.

There was a lot of tension and not much entertainment produced when the sides met. In terms of importance, games against them were nothing compared to our clashes with Real Madrid or Barcelona.

As part of our wage scheme, three fixtures gave us chances to double our win bonus money, which I thought was a good way to incentivise the team.

The players were allowed to pick one opponent and of course we usually picked what we thought would be an easy team. The directors chose the other two and inevitably they went for the league's biggest sides, Real Madrid and Barcelona.

The first time I played against Madrid it had been raining heavily for two days beforehand. There were puddles of water all over the pitch, yet the game went ahead. The conditions were ridiculous but I managed to score in a 2-1 win, which delighted all the fans, and of course the players.

We enjoyed even more success against Barcelona. In total I played against them six times, scoring eight goals with all but two of those coming in the Nou Camp. I also managed to score a winning goal against Atletico Madrid that guaranteed Barca the title.

A week later we played at the Nou Camp and beat the hosts comfortably, 3-1 the final score. They didn't mind and took us out celebrating with them in town afterwards.

On the road to Spain: A new life...

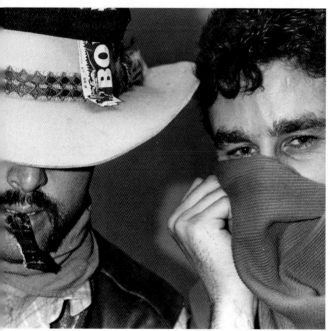

Guess who: In fancy dress with 'bounty hunter' Brucie Grobbelaar at a Liverpool Christmas party

Scoring when it matters: My reaction says it all after I have found the net in the semi-final replay against Forest in 1989. Below: More goals – against QPR

Liverpool Masters: Good team, but you can see we're all starting to lose it

Title toast: Steve McMahon gets a soaking as Peter Beardsley looks on

Irish highs: Once I broke my duck, the goals started to flow. Here I am (top and above) scoring both in the 2-0 win against Malta that secured our passage to Italia '90

Off duty: Relaxing in Dublin while with Ireland

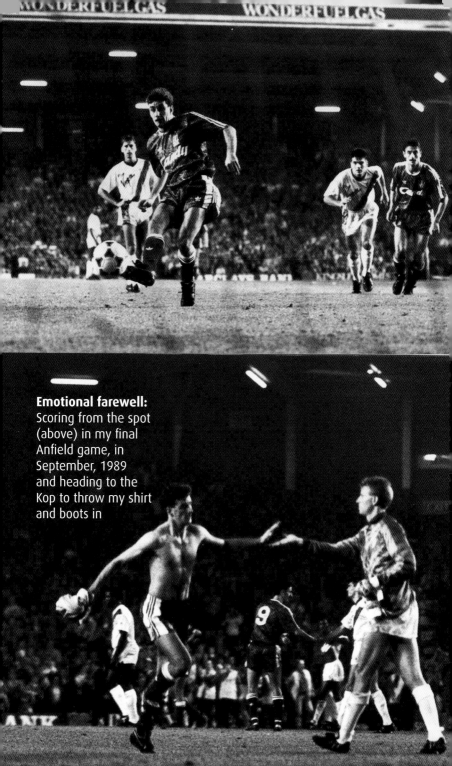

Emotional farewell:
Scoring from the spot
(above) in my final
Anfield game, in
September, 1989
and heading to the
Kop to throw my shirt
and boots in

Souvenirs: I've collected a few shirts from over the years, including Maradona's – and one from Germany's Stefan Kuntz!

Two of a kind: The old Rush and the new Rush – on a tour of the city with the FA Cup in 1989

Get in: You can't beat scoring in front of the Kop

The ball's in the net: Reminding a goalkeeper in Spain that I had just beaten him

On parade: The fans came to watch training at Real Sociedad, which took a bit of getting used to at first

Night out:
With Anfield team-mates on a pre-season tour of Scandinavia in July 1988 – note the dodgy '80s gear!

Kop family:
With the fans after scoring at Charlton, August 1988

ON-FIELD RIVALS – AND LOOK-ALIKES!

21/03/10, OLD TRAFFORD:

"Will you sign this book for me please?" says a woman just outside the pressroom deep within Manchester United's cavernous ground. "Of course," I reply, before looking down and realising what she wants me to scribble my autograph on. I pause before telling her: "I'm John Aldridge, not Ian Rush." She'd wanted me to sign Rushie's autobiography. I later discovered former United player Mickey Thomas, a friend of mine, had been behind the joke.

When I first heard Rushie was coming back to Liverpool I was absolutely gutted. I'd won the Golden Boot during that '87/88 season, scoring 29 goals and couldn't see why we needed another striker. Maybe Kenny didn't want him going to a different English club instead. Liverpool also took that stance when it came to signing players. The fans obviously wanted him back because he was a great player and rightly adored by everyone.

The problem was in his absence the style of play had changed. When Rushie had played previously most attacks had gone down the middle. Now it was all out wide with me getting on the end of crosses from the wings. He was no mug when it came to doing the same, but I thought it suited me better. I felt that it wasn't broken so there was no need to fix it. We'd played some brilliant football in '87/88, some people said we were the best ever Liverpool team to watch. Now the side was probably going to be altered.

But I'm a fighter and promised myself I'd keep going and do my best to earn my place. When the new season started I did that by scoring both goals in our 2-1 Charity Shield win over Wimbledon and a hat-trick at Charlton on the opening day of the league campaign. I eventually finished up with 31 goals and felt I could have done no more.

A quick glance at the top goalscorers from the 1988/89

season shows you that I had more than done my job of hitting the back of the net:

1988/89 Liverpool's top-scorers
1. Me – 31
2. John Barnes – 13
3. Peter Beardsley – 12
4. Ian Rush – 11
5. Ray Houghton – 7

Despite that, the following season Kenny told me I'd be better off going to Spain because I wouldn't be playing as much as I wanted. "Get the best deal you can," he said. That hurt, really hurt. When I did move on I got a letter from a 70-year-old Liverpool fan who'd followed the club since he was a kid. He said he wasn't going to go to any more matches because of the way I'd been treated. A fella from the Icelandic Supporters' club once asked me how I'd have felt if we'd sold Fernando Torres after his first season? "Hugely disappointed," I told him. His response: "That's how I felt after you left." An awful lot of people realised I'd been treated poorly. What more could I have done than score 63 goals in 104 games? Surely that was proof I was good enough.

Rushie's return might have meant the end for me but I never held that against him. Most people made a lot of the fact we looked similar, except the two of us. We never talked about it or mentioned it; there was no reason for us to do so. I've been mistaken for him on loads of occasions and vice versa.

Without a doubt Rushie was a magnificent player, even if I felt that he did get preferential treatment from the coaching staff sometimes.

There were many examples of it and one that always comes to mind involved shooting practice. Ronnie Moran was in charge of it with Brucie Grobbelaar in goal. The idea was to play a one-two with Ronnie and then score.

I put my effort wide and Ronnie shouted: "Aldo, hit the target." Ray Houghton was next up and he also put the ball wide. "Make the keeper work," Ronnie roared.

Rushie then stepped up and did the same. "Unlucky son, it happens in the game," was Ronnie's response.

It was an example of the respect everyone had for Ian, and with an incredible 346 goals for the club nobody could say he didn't deserve it.

... AND SOME OPPONENTS I ADMIRE

I rarely got a kick against big Paul McGrath, he was just too good. Playing against nobody else bothered me, no matter who it was it didn't faze me. I lined up against some of the best defenders around, guys like Franco Baresi and Paolo Maldini. But Paul was different, he was an incredible player.

I first faced him in the 1985/86 season when Oxford travelled to Old Trafford. We lost 3-0, he gave me a hard time and I remember having bruises afterwards from losing so many challenges against him.

We eventually became good mates during our time with Ireland. Everyone knows Paul was a great defender who read every situation so well. He didn't look it, but he was really quick too. You couldn't better him in any department and, because he was so good he never needed to break the rules. He was always fair. The levels he played at were incredible, especially when you consider what he went through off the field.

TEETOTAL NEV WAS WORLD CLASS TOO

On many occasions as a fan I'd witnessed how good Ray Clemence could be for Liverpool. He was the best keeper in the country and one of the reasons why so many trophies came to Anfield in the seventies and early eighties. He'd moved on to Spurs by the time I came up against him for Oxford. Even then he was still phenomenal.

However, he wasn't the best goalkeeper I ever faced, that

was Neville Southall. I'd place him just above Ray. The best save any keeper ever made from me was by Nev in a derby at Goodison. He was on the deck after pushing away a Peter Beardsley shot that was going into the bottom corner. I had a simple tap in, or so I thought.

When I hit it he spread himself superbly to make the block and I was left swearing and shaking my head. At the same time I said: "Well done". I still to this day don't know how he managed it.

The only shame was Wales never made it to the World Cup, because if they had I'm sure he'd have been recognised as one of the best keepers on the planet. As everyone knows he is a little different and can be pretty dour at times. He doesn't drink but I had a night out with him in Dublin once. We stayed out until four or five in the morning and he just drank Coca Cola the whole time. I couldn't do it, but that's Nev. His different approach to life never stopped him being brilliant.

RUBBING PEOPLE UP THE WRONG WAY

During our 1989 replayed FA Cup semi-final success over Nottingham Forest we produced some great football.

To end up on the winning side by a scoreline of 3-1 at the end was a very satisfying result, especially because of the difficult circumstances and it was also pleasing to score a brace of headers.

Forest defender Brian Laws' own goal completed our win. Just after he put the ball in the net, I celebrated by rubbing his head. Immediately I knew I'd gone too far and felt bad. Brian was rightly angry about it. Forest were also our next opponents in the league and I tried to make amends but Brian refused to accept my apology.

Since then there has been no problem between us, we get on well and I even wrote to the FA to try to help Brian's case when he got in trouble after an incident with Ivano Bonetti at Grimsby. I managed the player at Tranmere so knew how infuriating he could be. I was only happy to back up Brian as a way of apologising for what I'd done.

Some other people in the game didn't like my actions during that week in 1989, Tony Adams and Stuart Pearce chief amongst the group.

Adams, the Arsenal captain, is said to have rubbed my head just after they'd claimed the title at Anfield, mimicking what I did to Laws. I don't even remember it happening because we'd just missed out on the title but perhaps if he realised what I and all the players had been through after Hillsborough, then he would not have done it.

Pearce spoke out about it in his book and I didn't agree with him. The incident didn't involve him. Yet he felt it right to comment. I could do the same by commenting on his promotion with England ... but I won't.

EIGHT RIVAL TEAMS I FACED
1. *Everton*
2. *Manchester United*
3. *England*
4. *Arsenal*
5. *Athletic Bilbao*
6. *Barcelona*
7. *Real Madrid*
8. *Holland*

EIGHT ON-FIELD RIVALS I ADMIRE
1. *Paul McGrath*
2. *Rushie*
3. *Paolo Maldini*
4. *Ronald Koeman*
5. *Alan Hansen*
6. *Emilio Butragueno (in 1990-91, he beat me by one goal to the Pichichi, which is the trophy the Spanish newspaper Marca awards to the top league scorer)*
7. *Neville Southall*
8. *Dave Beasant*

WALK ON

- We played Oxford and battered them 6-0 and just before the end the Kop started singing 'Aldo is a Kopite'. He had a grin on his face wider than the Mersey

- I got tw*tted on the head by Aldo's left boot when he stripped in his final game and threw everything in the Kop (my mate still has the boot!)

- Aldo is a Liverpool legend. On and off the airwaves

- Thread from an unofficial LFC messageboard on the internet

JOHN ALDRIDGE

Liverpool-born Ian-Rush lookalike who finally arrived at Anfield via Newport and Oxford, who Liverpool paid £750,000 in January 1987. Scored in eleven successive League starts for Liverpool.

A LOVE AFFAIR STARTS WITH A REJECTION

Saturday, January 21, 1967. 47,545 people officially attended Anfield to watch Bill Shankly's team, the defending champions, face a Southampton side that were competing in English football's highest division for the very first time.

None of those inside the stadium that day could have been as happy as me, it just wasn't possible.

I was eight-years-old and, as we made our way to the paddock area of the Main Stand, life couldn't have been any better. My dad and uncle had brought me along for my debut at the famous ground and ignited a passion that remains inside me. Chris Lawler and Alf Arrowsmith scored in the space of 12 first half minutes to help earn a 2-1 win.

In truth I didn't pay much attention to what was happening on the field. My gaze was fully focused on something else, a wall of noise, colour, wit and emotion.

There to my right was the Kop and even before kick-off it had left me shocked. As a youngster I'd never seen anything else to compare to it and, despite the passing of many years, I still haven't. It was an instant addiction. I wanted to go back every week to watch just that, rather than 22 players kicking a ball.

It was my ambition to become part of such an amazing choir. My dad wasn't sure about that plan. He rightly felt I was still too small to be in with the Reds' hardcore fans on my own. Thankfully my uncle Tommy Cain was only too happy to come to my aid. I'd catch the bus from Garston and arrive outside the ground at half one.

Once inside we'd get a decent spec with a barrier behind me. Watching live football and playing it all the time meant my main ambition in life soon centred on becoming one of Shankly's team.

I had some potential, but nothing compared to one player I faced when playing for the school. Immediately this lad stood out from the rest and you could see he would have a career in the game. His name was Sammy Lee. For me progress wasn't so assured.

At the age of roughly 14, I went for trials at Liverpool, which had come about courtesy of our local gasman, a man called Johnny Bennison, who scouted for Liverpool in his spare time. I must have impressed someone because I was soon training with the club on Tuesdays and Thursdays.

The pride and satisfaction that brought me disappeared in a second when Tom Saunders, the man in charge of the youth set-up told me they'd be letting me go after only a few months. I was completely devastated and then equally delighted when they invited me for another trial a year or so later after my dad had pestered them to do so.

I scored a few goals and I can remember Tom sitting us down after we'd been there for about six weeks. He said to one lad: "Sorry, you haven't made it" and then to another "excellent today – I'll see you in two weeks' time".

Then he came to me. He said: "Great goal today John (I had scored our consolation against the 'B' team in a heavy defeat). We'll definitely be giving you a ring".

I waited and waited for that call to come but it never did. Indeed, I had to wait 14 years and it ended up costing the club £750,000 – that's the fee Liverpool paid Oxford to sign me. I don't remember the names of anyone else who attended those trials so Liverpool probably made the right decisions on most of those youngsters. With me they certainly didn't.

HAIR-RAISING DAY BUT REDS A CUT ABOVE

Not even cruel rejections could crush my affection for the Liverbird. While those in the recruitment section of the club were trying to push me away the first team were drawing me in deeper.

I regularly went and stood on the Kop. It was a brilliant place to be, even if a fellow Kopite once mistook me for a girl because of my long hair. He was a massive bloke, probably a docker or a boxer, and whenever the crowd moved forward I could feel him pressed up against me. I was convinced he was going to roll up an Echo and piss on me. But when the heaving throng moved backwards and I had some space he turned to me and said: 'Sorry, love'. I went straight to the barbers the next day.

A fright like that didn't stop me going to Anfield and I also attended away fixtures whenever I could. It was the best time to be a fan. We were spoilt. Trophies came along every May. It's unimaginable now, but winning the league didn't bring about any huge fanfare. We didn't, but it felt like we won it every year. It was natural, a part of our annual routine.

That attitude was still in place even when I was part of the title winning squad in 1988. It just wasn't a big deal for any Liverpool player or supporter. Now I think we'd be partying non-stop for a year if the team became champions. Back then we were all blasé about it. If it didn't happen it felt unusual.

GREAT EXPECTATIONS

I recall a story that sums up how fans' attitudes have changed since those days. When I was at Newport, I came back to Liverpool and met up with a good friend of mine when I was growing up called Alan Abbott. We were in Speke market one day and I asked him if he was still going to the games at Anfield.

He said: "Nah – I don't enjoy it now. You just get sick of winning things. I'd rather be at the bottom of the league fighting relegation".

It's quite interesting to sit here now and think back to that time when the trophies rolled in on a regular basis and the fans expected success. I bet if I caught up with Alan now, after the club's struggles on and off the pitch over the intervening years, he wouldn't be taking things for granted like he did back in those days.

A long time without winning the league then was seven

years, between 1964 and 1973. I attended the game against Leicester City, a 0-0 draw, when that 'famine' was ended. Going over 20 years without winning it was something none of us would have ever comprehended. We were too busy enjoying ourselves.

Victories were important, the fact they were achieved with style and drama made it all even better. Coming from behind to beat the likes of Bruges and St. Etienne are fabulous memories for me. The team seemed to almost relish being in a difficult situation that needed rescuing. As fans we revelled in it too.

Now and again there were some deficits we couldn't overturn, such as at Wembley in 1977. I'd travelled down to London for the FA Cup final against Tommy Docherty's Manchester United. Jimmy Case cancelled out Stuart Pearson's opener in fantastic style. For me Jimmy's goal is one of the best ever in the cup final.

He was from the Allerton and Garston area, not far from where I lived, and played for the Blue Union amateur team a few years before I did. I once met him in a local pub at Christmas. Despite the fact he was a Liverpool player, he stayed out for quite a few pints and we had a great laugh. Unfortunately Jimmy's goal wasn't enough to prevent a 2-1 defeat thanks to a rather fortunate deflected winner for the Mancs.

The result ended our hopes of a treble for Bob Paisley and it hurt. On the way home we were all really down, with the biggest fear being that the team would find it so difficult to lift themselves for the European Cup final in Rome a few days later. Thankfully that wasn't a problem as Terry McDermott, THAT Tommy Smith header and Phil Neal's penalty provided a 3-1 win over Borussia Monchengladbach to make us champions of Europe for the very first time.

Twelve months later, I was back at Wembley to watch us retain 'Big Ears' in style thanks to Kenny Dalglish's brilliant chipped finish against Bruges.

A load of us had gone to the capital on a mini-bus, before making our way to Leicester Square to start on the ale. It was last orders by the time we got to the pubs afterwards.

Our only option was to buy a load of cans for the celebrations on the bus home. I remember all the banter before and afterwards but not much of what happened on the pitch. We didn't care, as long as we won.

I FINISHED A LIVERPOOL LEGEND'S CAREER

As much as I enjoyed watching my heroes, and everything that went with it, I eventually had to stop attending so many games. I was playing every weekend myself, for sides such as Garston Woodcutters and Cheshire Lines before I joined semi-professional team South Liverpool and moved from there to Newport County in 1979. Even in my absence the trophies kept coming to Anfield. Usually it meant going to my local to watch the games instead of attending the match; that involved many days in the pub such as the League Cup finals and the European Cup finals.

I watched the '81 win in Paris courtesy of Alan Kennedy's great goal in my local. Thankfully when I was sold by Newport to Oxford United near the end of 1983/84 our season had finished and I was again able to watch the game with Roma back in Liverpool. The pub was rammed and I have to admit I didn't think we'd win when it went to penalties. As the home side I fancied Roma to succeed in the shootout.

That was before I knew about what Bruce Grobbelaar had planned. Only he could have come up with that idea. We were all laughing at him because he looked stupid when he first started wobbling and dancing.

Obviously it worked very well. Having taken many penalties I know something like that can have an affect. It takes your focus off the job. If a keeper had done that to me I would have been thinking 'what is he up to?' Having got to know him later on, Brucie simply didn't care what people thought about him or his actions. At Melwood he'd turn up for training and not really bother. He just played outfield in the five-a-side games. He never stayed behind for extra sessions either. I did to work on my finishing, usually with Peter Beardsley in goal.

Bruce was a very talented keeper. And I'm sure his madness played a part in Bruno Conti and Francesco Grazini firing over the bar for the hosts. It meant Alan Kennedy, again, had the chance to score a European Cup final winner.

To do it once is fantastic for anyone. Scoring the winner in club football's biggest game twice is a phenomenal achievement. Alan is a good bloke and a very good friend of mine. We always have a laugh when we meet up, particularly when I remind him of how I helped end his Liverpool career in a game at the Manor Ground.

I'd opened the scoring for Oxford with a header. After the interval Rushie and Craig Johnston scored to give them a 2-1 lead. Time was running out when I put Alan under pressure by chasing a long ball. At first he tried to shepherd it back to safety. Then he opted to knock it back towards the keeper, with far too much pace. It went over Bruce's head and finished in the net. Alan never wore the Red shirt again. He mightn't recall the day fondly. I do, and that night out. Loads of my family and friends had travelled down for the game; I had a tough time trying to satisfy their ticket demands. Providing accommodation, albeit a little cramped, wasn't such a problem. They all stayed at mine.

Alan tells a story now about that back pass incident. When the ball went over the line, he says, there was an answer message left on a phone in the goal by Bruce saying: "Sorry, I'm not in at the moment – I'll be back soon!" That summed Bruce up. He was a fantastic keeper but quite often you didn't know where he'd get to.

Our first four European Cup finals produced great nights and unforgettable triumphs. 1985 is also something that will remain in our memories for a long time, for all the wrong reasons. Again I managed to get back to Merseyside to watch it, this time in the Hunts Cross pub.

I remember we were all shocked by what was on unfolding on the TV screen in front of us. We couldn't believe it was our fans involved and that 39 Italians had passed away. Everyone was very upset and people in the pub started arguing about who had actually caused the trouble in the stadium. It got so heated we decided to leave.

On the way home the fact that people had died at a game dominated my thoughts, it was a very sad night for all of us. The game itself should never have been played, we all know that and I think it's a disgrace that UEFA insisted that it go ahead.

I was pleased to see Liverpool erect a memorial to the tragedy in the summer of 2010. It was something that they should have done a long time ago.

THE GREATEST MANAGER? NO DOUBT...

The vast majority of the honours that Liverpool won when I was growing up came during the reigns of Bill Shankly and Bob Paisley. Bob won more trophies, including a hat-trick of European Cups, but for me there is no question about who was greater.

Shanks had arrived when the club was in serious trouble, not even in the First Division. They were going nowhere. He used his personality and character to create something special.

He was an honest and determined man who I simply adored. We need someone like that again now, someone to inspire and rebuild the club from top to bottom.

Joe Fagan was also a very good manager who time seems to have forgotten. He was only in charge for two seasons and reached the European Cup final in both of those.

Winning three trophies in his first year in charge was a brilliant achievement that he deserved more praise for. I only ever met Joe a few times and on occasion he came across as a real gentleman.

SINGING MY NAME

By the time I started coming up against Liverpool at Oxford Kenny Dalglish had succeeded Joe.

The standard of the football remained just as impressive as what I'd watched on a regular basis. I had a close-up confirmation of this on the first occasion I played at Anfield. Within a minute Rushie had scored. By half-time it was 3-0 and the deficit had doubled at the end. Liverpool could, and probably should, have reached double figures.

Despite us getting destroyed I did enjoy some moments of the afternoon. The Kop sang my name after I'd appeared on BBC beforehand talking about my affection for LFC. Hearing the stand I'd been part of praise me had been part of my childhood dreams, although obviously I was on the other team scoring goals when I'd imagined it happening.

The Reds finished that season by winning the double and I watched with great joy. For Kenny to do so much as player-manager was brilliant. As I say, I had contemplated going to the first all-Merseyside FA Cup final and was given tickets by Oxford. But because I hadn't been to any of the games leading up to the final, I thought it was only right that I gave them to friends and relatives who had attended the earlier rounds, especially with it being such a special occasion.

I watched it in our house in Oxford while drinking a few cans of beer. Naturally I enjoyed it, even if I regretted not going to Wembley. That night I went out celebrating. Bizarrely there were quite a few Liverpool fans around the part of Oxford where we lived, so we had a great time. It wasn't long before my team were making me suffer again though. That October I played at Anfield again. Once more it ended in a heavy defeat, although this time it was only 4-0.

'YOU'RE OFF TO LIVERPOOL'

Next time I ran past the 'This Is Anfield' sign I was wearing red. The news that my fantasy would become a reality first reached me on January 3, 1987.

Oxford were due to face Man City at Maine Road that afternoon. On the morning of the game my room-mate Bobby McDonald finished talking on the phone and said Maurice Evans, the manager, wanted to see me. "You're off to Liverpool," Bobby joked.

Arsenal had been constantly named as one of the sides who wanted to sign me. It was also obvious that Ian Rush was on his way to Serie A and would need to be replaced. Being the man to do that job naturally appealed, even if I never dared to think it would actually happen. Thankfully they were the side who wanted to buy me. When Maurice told me my head immediately started spinning. Having waited so long to be a Liverpool player I wanted the deal to be done instantly. I couldn't think about our match which was going to take place in a few hours.

When I did get out on the pitch I just couldn't focus properly. Nothing else mattered apart from officially signing for my club. Agonisingly I had to wait until the end of the month before everything fell into place. After thinking about it for years, a few more weeks shouldn't have made much difference. But it wasn't good for my state of mind. As much as playing my last game for Oxford saddened me, I was finally going where I always wanted to be. Joan was just as pleased because we were going back home.

A return to familiar surroundings was accompanied by a new role for me, that of substitute. My first involvement, which I'd waited so long for, came against Aston Villa away, towards the end of February. We were out of the FA Cup and I was ineligible for the League Cup because I'd already played in it at Oxford. Paul Walsh's sending off in the same competition meant a ban and a start for me in our next league game, Southampton's visit to Anfield. This was what I'd hoped for. As much as being part of the squad was special, I wanted to be in the team. I responded by scoring the afternoon's solitary goal with a header past Peter Shilton after Jan Molby had delivered a great free kick into the box.

The roar from the crowd as the ball went in the net was immense. It was a magical moment and as good as all those thousands of times I'd imagined it.

However, I wouldn't repeat it, or even start again, until the last day of the season. 10 times I sat on the bench and in three of those I didn't even get on the pitch. I was worried. Kenny assured me I was part of his plans, but for the following season when Rushie had gone to Juventus.

1987-88

Those words from the boss proved to be true. That summer was one of reconstruction on and off the field.

A collapsed Victorian drain under the Kop meant the builders had to be called in and we couldn't play at home until September 12, against Oxford United. I had to put my affection for my former team to one side as I scored the opening goal in a 2-0 win.

That was part of my fabulous beginning to the season when I found the net in our first nine league outings. The impact of new arrivals John Barnes and Peter Beardsley for large sums of money was a significant factor in our form. Ray Houghton followed in October. We produced brilliant, breathtaking football. The goals were flying in and nobody could cope with us. It was what I'd hoped for as a kid. It was nearly perfect.

Barnesie won the PFA Player of the Year award and we accumulated 90 points. He was unbelievable and Liverpool haven't had anyone like him since then. In all competitions we only lost four times.

Our neighbours, the reigning champions, knocked us out of the League Cup and also ended our 29 game unbeaten league run that had equalled the best ever start by a team in the top division.

Leeds had also gone 29 games undefeated in 1973/74, a sequence that was only bettered when Arsenal went unbeaten for the whole of 2003/04. Our only other league defeat came at the City Ground in April.

And we gained a swift and stylish revenge for that later the same month.

The legendary Tom Finney said our 5-0 win over Brian Clough's side on the night of April 13 was: "The finest exhibition I've seen the whole time I've played and watched the game. You couldn't see it bettered anywhere, not even in Brazil. The moves they put together were fantastic."

BBC Radio's Alan Green commented: "That was simply the best display of an exceptional season from Liverpool. Reporters are often accused, rightly, of being too glib of using words like brilliant, fantastic, fabulous. Liverpool deserved all these adjectives tonight."

Others said it reminded them of the fantastic Real Madrid team which won the European Cup five years in a row. For me Tom Finney's comments meant the most, he was so well respected and had obviously seen so much football. I might have been out on the pitch but it was the best Liverpool performance I've ever seen too. You have to put wins like that into context and Forest were a good side who finished third that season and had beaten us.

Strangely we hadn't played that well during the first 15 minutes of the evening. Then we clicked as a team and they just couldn't stop us. I got two on the night and Peter Beardsley's pass for my opening goal was phenomenal. I couldn't have asked for a better through ball and chipped it over the keeper as he went down.

Kenny taught me to do that. He always said when the keeper came out and spread himself the best way to beat him was to just dink the ball over him. That put us two goals up and we played some brilliant football from then on. Ray Houghton, Gary Gillespie and Peter were the others on the scoresheet and the rest of the lads could have had a few too. When you're part of a team performance like that you know it's good. You try things you wouldn't normally try and everything comes off. Forest didn't know how to stop us, Afterwards Neil Webb said to me: "There is nothing you can do about that."

Our passing and moving was exceptional, especially when you consider most of us had been on the ale at the PFA Awards dinner a few days earlier. On a personal note it was great to do that against a team that contained Stuart Pearce. He hated Steve McMahon, so to rub his nose in it was great.

REGRETS...

"Put up your hands up and block him," I always scream when I see footage of John Lukic about to bowl the ball out to Lee Dixon at Anfield on that night in May 1989 when they snatched the title away from us at the latest possible moment.

I knew Barnesie was still out of position so I should have stopped the keeper to slow down the play. It would have meant a booking, but so what.

If I had done it, Michael Thomas' chance probably wouldn't have been created and we would have won the double. Two years on the run we were so close to finishing with both trophies. To not do it on either occasion is one of my biggest footballing regrets.

My penalty miss obviously made a difference in '88. Although there was no guarantee we would have gone on to win, even if I had scored. Twelve months on, we were a lot closer. If we had hung on for just another minute it would have been ours.

We wanted it to add to the FA Cup and help honour those who had passed away at Hillsborough.

'DON'T UNDERSELL YOURSELF'
Sometimes, no matter how badly you don't want something to happen, there is little you can do to prevent it. It's hugely frustrating but, eventually, you just have to try your best to

salvage something from the situation. Everybody knows I never wanted to leave Liverpool in September 1989.

I would have happily stayed there forever. However, it appeared everything had fallen into place to facilitate my departure from the club I loved. Even though we were mates and had proved we could play together Rushie's return was never going to be good news for me. I was always aware of that. Falling out with Kenny Dalglish when he made me play two games in one day didn't do me any favours either.

All the indications were that my time at Anfield was about to come to a halt. I didn't want that and at first refused to believe it was going to happen. Before long, though, I had to be realistic and accept my future lay elsewhere, playing for another club. I also knew if I wanted to be involved in the following summer's World Cup with Ireland, I needed to be playing regularly.

Not starting in the Charity Shield win over Arsenal at Wembley was something I'd have to get used to in my last few weeks as a Red. When we faced Man City and Aston Villa in our opening league games I was also left sitting on the bench. I eventually got to play, for the final 17 minutes of our scoreless match with Luton at Kenilworth Road. It was a depressing and worrying time for me.

A few days after that draw we all flew to Spain for a glamour game with Real Madrid in the Bernabeu and it became obvious that, although I didn't know what my next career move would be, others did. It was no shock to find myself a sub again in a 2-0 defeat against the famous Spaniards.

Afterwards I spotted Peter Robinson and John Smith chatting with men who I had learned were from Real Sociedad. I was confused and wanted to know what was going on so I interrupted their discussions, even though I didn't receive any straight answers.

When I got back to Liverpool I asked Kenny about it and he told me the talks between the clubs were ongoing.

His advice was: "Don't undersell yourself." The manager had obviously given up on keeping me and there was no point in me arguing with him again. As it all slowly sank in that I was leaving I was devastated.

AN EMOTIONAL NIGHT

By the time Crystal Palace arrived at Anfield for a midweek game on September 12 every man and his dog in the city knew I was on my way to Sociedad for £1.15m. Like me, the people on the streets couldn't believe it either, plenty of them have told me exactly that since then. I wanted to get on the pitch to say my farewells to those fans that had treated me brilliantly but I knew I'd be on the bench.

Putting me on from the start probably wasn't the Liverpool way. Kenny had made me play two games in one day so he was never going to put me in the first eleven just because I was leaving. Instead he stuck with Peter and Rushie up front while I watched from the sidelines as the lads battered a poor Palace team.

Even when you take the standard of opposition into account, the lads performed brilliantly and following some early goals Palace simply gave up. It was 5-0 just after the hour mark. Reaching double figures looked likely at that point; all I wanted was the chance to get one goal.

Thankfully it came my way when we were awarded a penalty after 66 minutes. It was a nice gesture from Kenny to send me on as a substitute and I got immense pleasure in putting the ball in the net from 12 yards. I know Kenny didn't have to bring me on but I thought I deserved that moment to score after what I'd done for the club. Before the end we added three more to record a 9-0 win.

At the final whistle I didn't really know what was going on or what to do. Throwing my shirt into the Kop, followed by my socks and boots, was completely unplanned. Partially because I was emotional and partially because I'd already taken off most of my kit, I didn't remain on the pitch for too long.

The fans gave me a standing ovation and the lads applauded me too. Back in the dressing room, I had a massive lump in my throat and I had to lock myself in the toilet for a few minutes to compose myself.

Suddenly I wasn't a Liverpool player any more. Something that I'd wanted so badly for so long had been taken away from me against my will. I'd lived my dream, had a stint at my club and it was now over.

I had a few beers that night, just a few because I knew I was going to Spain to be unveiled as a Sociedad signing later that week. I couldn't hang around. I'd scored 63 goals in 104 games for Liverpool. That was me doing my job as far as I was concerned. For others it obviously wasn't good enough.

ANYONE BUT LIVERPOOL?

After my departure a part of me didn't want Liverpool to win any more. I found that strange because it was the only time I'd felt that way. Thankfully that bitterness wore off eventually. I even returned to Anfield again to see the lads.

It was a good idea, even if it was a strange experience. Thankfully I'd got on well with all my team-mates and they welcomed me back. Any time any of us had ever had a disagreement or a bust up we'd always shaken hands and sorted it out afterwards. There were never any grudges held. I felt very comfortable being in their presence. Being back at the ground was not a nice feeling though. It reinforced how big the club was and the fact that I wasn't involved there any more.

YOU CAN'T BEAT PASSION

My Anfield career might have ended badly but there were plenty of great moments prior to its conclusion. Singling out just one is almost impossible, every game was huge. I think that's one of the reasons why I loved it. I won League and FA Cup medals in my time there, with the Cup win in '89 being really important for the fans after what had happened at

Hillsborough. I've been lucky. At Newport and Oxford I also won medals. Many players never win any; I finished with plenty including Golden Boots too.

The biggest honour I could ever have had wasn't any of those; it was wearing that red shirt. Being local I think you feel it more than those from outside the city. I'm not saying other players from elsewhere don't have a passion for Liverpool. They do. But it meant more to me because I'd grown up watching the team, home and away. It was something I'd wanted for a long time. They grew to like the club because they joined it. I already loved it and would have even if I hadn't played for Liverpool.

I look at some players now and wonder if they have any understanding of what LFC means to the fans. They prance around, don't show commitment and then leave with a pile of cash. I think, no matter where they come from, it's important that young players know what the club is all about.

The history and what they are playing for is vital. John McMahon sat his reserve team lads down at the start of the 2009/10 season and showed them a DVD to explain the foundations of the club. It was a good move because some of them probably didn't have a clue about it.

STICKING UP FOR STEVIE AND CARRA
Two of our most important players in recent years are a duo that you could never say the same about. I watch Steven Gerrard and Jamie Carragher very closely; they have been the heartbeat of the team for a long time.

You can see them put in just that little bit more than others, they go to the point where they will gladly get hurt to help the cause. People know they are obviously from the city and that puts the onus on them in particular for the team to deliver success. I was always aware of that element but it didn't worry me. We were a very successful side in my two years there so there was never much criticism. Even after I missed the penalty people never said too much.

I've met the lads and spoken to them quite a few times. They understand the pressure that goes with being a local player. It can lead to unfair criticism and I've always backed the two of them up when I hear people having a go at them. Steven got a lot of stick when he scored that own goal against Chelsea in the 2005 Carling Cup final. It was just the frustration of fans because we had been so close to winning the match. I spoke up for him on the radio afterwards.

The next day Steve phoned me and thanked me for backing him. That was something he didn't have to do. He rang me on my 50th birthday a few years ago too, calling me an 'old bastard!' I didn't need reminding of the fact I'd reached a half century of years but it was a nice gesture from him. Respect is a great thing in life.

When I first started working on the radio I couldn't believe how much criticism Jamie got. I could see he was a decent player who was giving his all.

On the phone-ins he was getting slaughtered for about a year. Then it started to change. He dealt with everything that came his way. He showed great character in doing so.

Problems such as deceitful American owners are also an extra burden for the local lads to deal with. I know if I was playing for Liverpool it would have affected me. The lads love the club and worrying about the future of it is a pressure that the other players normally don't have to deal with.

I am certain there will probably come a point in the future where there are no local lads in the first team. It will be a sad time for all of us. It's the way football has gone. Some people say it's a good thing, I disagree. We need that connection between city and club.

As far as I am concerned, the Premier League ruling – that from 2010, eight members of a 25-man squad must be 'home-grown' players – is a must. It can only be a good thing.

WATCHING FROM AFAR

Even when I lived in Spain I still kept up to date with Liverpool's fortunes. It was unavoidable really because a lot of my mates would always call me to let me know the latest news and results. My phone didn't stop ringing the night the lads drew 4-4 with Everton at Goodison Park in February 1991. It was shocking to hear they'd conceded so many goals. I was even more stunned when Kenny resigned the next day. Having spent five years as a manager myself I now know that it can get to you. You're passionate and love a club and it takes a lot out of you. When you add in what happened at Hillsborough that was probably the situation with Kenny. He clearly needed a break.

As we're all aware the club has never returned to the top position again and when I look back now I could see some cracks were starting to emerge even in my time there. Individuals like Jockey (Hansen) were getting older. Around the end of the '80s and early '90s the club signed a lot of players who weren't top class.

Lads like my mate Glenn Hysen and Ronny Rosenthal are great blokes, but they'd probably admit themselves that they weren't top class footballers. It was strange not to see the club bring in bigger names. I know they had signed Ray Houghton and me from Oxford in 1987 but John Barnes and Peter Beardsley, England regulars, also came in at that time. The club had seemed in an invincible position.

Within a few years that was all gone and other teams had taken over at the top of English football. It hurt me to see that situation developing. Graeme Souness, a hero of mine and one of the best players we've ever had, came in and probably tried to change too much. He let too many experienced players move on and signed some poor individuals to replace them. It was tough for me to watch the club fall so far in such a short space of time. When I came back to Tranmere I was always looking out for Liverpool results straight after our own games. And on most occasions it wasn't good news.

I think John Toshack would have been a better choice to keep the club going in the right direction. I got to know John in Spain and he can come across as a little arrogant at first. But he knew his stuff and usually did a good job for whatever team he was at.

I remember him telling me that he had been in for the Liverpool job once but instead the people in charge decided to make Joe Fagan the manager. They didn't even let Tosh know that the decision had been made. He was very angry and annoyed by the way they treated him. Then, I think it was after Kenny left, they asked him to take charge again. He agreed before changing his mind and not telling them. The club had treated him badly in the first place so Tosh didn't feel he owed them anything and wanted to get his own back on the people who had lied to him.

I SHOULD HAVE GONE WITH MY GUT INSTINCT

There was never much chance of me being on the winning side against Liverpool when I was at Newport or Oxford. But as manager of Tranmere I really believed my team could defeat Liverpool when we were drawn against them in the quarter-final of the 2001 FA Cup. And it would have given me great pleasure if we had won.

The Reds might have been the team I'd supported all my life, but eliminating them would have put us into the semi-finals. It would have been a huge achievement and we thought we could do it. The game came after we'd beaten Southampton in that ludicrous tie when we were three goals behind. Gerard Houllier had been at Prenton Park that famous night and he knew what to expect. Like a lot of Kopites he was rightly worried and didn't want to risk any foreign players in his starting line-up.

My own tactics were something that I was unsure about. We'd beaten Everton by playing 3-5-2. The question was should we go with that again or switch to 4-4-2. I had a meeting with my staff to decide what to do.

Liverpool were certain to play Robbie Fowler and Michael Owen up front. Both of them were small so that meant we could let them have possession out wide because chances were neither of the lads would score from a high cross. That was my logic and why I was leaning towards 3-5-2. It would have made us really solid down the middle, where the majority of Liverpool's goals eventually came from.

We all voted on it, with 4-4-2 being the option the majority chose. I know if we had used 3-5-2 instead we would have done well. It was a formation we were comfortable with. I look back on it now and think I should have been my own man and went with my instinct.

In the end we gave Liverpool some frights along the way before losing 4-2. In particular I remember when we'd just got it back to 3-2 and I put Dave Challinor on. His long throws were a great weapon and you could see the fear appear on the faces of Gerard, Thommo and Sammy Lee. Liverpool got Wycombe in the semi-final so if we had knocked them out we would have had a great chance of reaching Cardiff.

MY SON'S NEVER G-OWEN TO FORGIVE ME!

Along with my son Paul, I did go to the final to watch Liverpool face Arsenal in the Welsh capital. It was a scorching day and Arsene Wenger's team absolutely battered us. Somehow, mainly thanks to Stephane Henchoz's hand and some poor finishing, we only conceded one goal.

We left when it was 1-0 and thought there could only be one result. We were barely out of the ground when a roar went up and at first we thought it was 2-0. Then we discovered Michael Owen had made it 1-1 and Paul wanted to go back inside. I persuaded him to just go home as I figured Arsenal would surely score a winner. He's never forgiven me for causing him to miss one of our most dramatic cup final wins ever. Michael Owen ensured his place in Liverpool history that day, even if he has tarnished his reputation in our eyes since then by joining United in 2009.

ISTANBUL – A WEEK OF CELEBRATIONS

I thought winning a cup in dramatic circumstances couldn't be better than the efforts we witnessed in 2001. I was happy to be proved wrong just over four years later. Nobody – Red, blue or Manc – needs telling what happened in Istanbul. It was a breathtaking night. I was left almost speechless on Radio City.

I think I had a sore throat for days afterwards because I'd shouted so much, first in frustration and then in joy at the end as we secured our fifth European Cup. The bad throat might have had something to do with the celebratory drinks I had too. We couldn't get a beer in the stadium. By the time we finished the broadcast and left it was 2am. We made up for it back at the hotel. There were loads of Reds there, including Gary Gillespie and, the sadly deceased since then, Phil Easton from Radio City.

We had a big sing-song. My son came in carrying a huge banner in the middle of what turned out to be a great session that continued until morning time.

A fella who'd left the stadium at half time with his son even turned up. He was able to laugh about it and so was I as I'd learned my lesson about leaving early in Cardiff. I don't think the radio station would have been too happy either if I had downed tools at half-time.

When we got to the airport the next day we had a couple of drinks to celebrate and tried to get through the crowds. But all the flights had been delayed.

Thousands and thousands of Liverpool fans were there. They spotted me and lifted me high above the crowd while singing and celebrating, it was fantastic. I was honoured and privileged to receive such treatment from my fellow Kopites.

The best thing was they carried me to the front of the queue where I was able to walk straight on to my plane, start drinking again and depart after just a few minutes!

The few beers carried on until Manchester airport. Then I phoned my missus up and told her I was still stuck in Turkey before I went out for a few more pints in Liverpool.

It was only a white lie and she didn't mind when I told her the real story. I went to my bar in town. Then I went to the Sir Thomas Hotel across the road to meet up with Xabi Alonso, Steven Gerrard, Dietmar Hamann and all the players.

After the hotel we went back to our bar again for a lock-in. Brian McFadden came in and was singing on the bar. That night after was better than the night of the game for celebrations.

Even the next day we were all out again, I think it went on for a week in total.

PART OF THE LIVERPOOL FAMILY

Those festivities confirmed to me that once you are a part of the Liverpool family it never leaves you. I'd gone from the club nearly 16 years earlier yet it still felt like I was one of the players. Other ex-Reds will agree with me. All I can say is it's like a society, similar to the Masons. There is a bond and whenever we all meet up, even if we never played together, we get on famously.

Anfield plays a big part in that. Whenever I walk in there I get a buzz. The respect I receive from the fans, especially the older fans, is brilliant because they remember me playing.

Our side from 1988 was probably the most flamboyant Liverpool team ever, we expressed ourselves brilliantly. It's hard to say we were the best ever Liverpool team because we didn't win the European Cup. I think we'd have had a great chance if we had competed for it.

For me the best team I've seen was the side of the late '70s, they were brilliant and won that competition two years in a row.

They were what helped fuel my footballing ambitions, the most important of which I achieved by wearing a Liverbird on my shirt.

EIGHT OF MY FAVOURITE LIVERPOOL PLAYERS
(In no particular order – and it's not an easy choice!)
1. *Graeme Souness*
2. *Terry McDermott*
3. *Tommy Smith*
4. *Emlyn Hughes*
5. *Kenny Dalglish*
6. *Roger Hunt*
7. *Ian Rush*
8. *Steven Gerrard*

EIGHT TROPHIES I'VE SEEN LIVERPOOL WIN LIVE
1972/73 League title
1975/76 UEFA CUP
1976/77 League title
1977/78 European Cup
2000/01 UEFA CUP
2002/03 League Cup
2004/05 European Cup/Champions League
2005/06 FA Cup

MY EIGHT FAVOURITE SCOUSE REDS
Jamie Carragher *
Steven Gerrard
Jimmy Case
Terry McDermott
Robbie Fowler
Steve McMahon
Sammy Lee
Dave Johnson

* I don't know why but for some reason I once left him out of a Scouse XI I picked. That was a mistake.

CHAPTER 5: STICKING TOGETHER

TEAM SPIRIT

'Peter Reid said he drank vodka and mouthwash when he ran out of mixer. Can you top that?'

*'F***ing hell! I'm not a shorts man, don't go anywhere near shots or anything like that. I once had pints of vodka and Red Bull in Magaluf with the Tranmere lads. We started at three in the afternoon and were still on it at five in the morning. I ended up with a terrible headache and wanted to go to sleep, but the Red Bull wouldn't let me drop off. It was horrible, awful. Never again...'*

Interview from FourFourTwo Magazine

A picture from my Newport days, celebrating promotion in 1980 and (top) a cutting from a Liverpool fancy dress party...

WHY JASON REALLY HAD A BUST-UP WITH ROY

Ireland's pre-World Cup training camp, Saipan, May 2002:

Jason McAteer answered a knock on his bedroom door and found Roy Keane waiting there. The skipper had called to borrow a blue movie. As the squad's 'head of 'entertainment' Jason was usually the person the players turned to in times of such need.

"Because it was Roy I had to hand over my best bluey," Jason told me later on. "I didn't want to be giving him any old rubbish." The following day it all kicked off and Roy was on his way home – without returning what he'd borrowed. I think that was why they clashed in the Sunderland versus Manchester United game at the Stadium of Light later that year... because Jason wanted the video back.

Apart from loaning out videos, Jason's role as one of the senior players meant he usually tried to keep team spirits up. Looking at what happened, though, it's obvious there wasn't much harmony in the Irish squad during the build-up to the World Cup in Japan and Korea. There were always bust-ups in every group of players I was part of. It's up to the manager and his staff to sort it out. I thought it was handled badly in 2002 and what went on should never have reached the media. If Jack Charlton had been in charge everything would have been kept in-house. It wasn't, it leaked out. Some people say Mick McCarthy let it out deliberately because he wanted to put pressure on Roy. Roy can be impetuous and could fly off the wall. That's what he did.

It was a very sad event. The biggest loser wasn't Mick or Roy; it was Irish football. I still believe we could have got to the semi-finals of that competition at least.

Had we knocked out Spain, which we nearly did, that side of the draw was wide open and the lads could have made it to the last four. I think later in life Roy will regret the fact that he didn't get to play in that tournament.

The most successful teams usually need to have a great spirit and sense of camaraderie. It's not always easy to build. Whereever I played, our usual method of creating such an atmosphere involved going for a few drinks.

LIVERPOOL NIGHTS OUT

Back in the '80s, Liverpool would always let us have nights out, with the highlight being the fancy dress Christmas party.

Not many managers would go out with their players but Kenny Dalglish did. One year he turned up dressed as a judge. This was just after Jan Molby had made a few appearances in court and been locked up. John Barnes memorably wore a Ku Klux Klan costume too. Nothing was really off limits and the media never picked up that story...

I wasn't quite so controversial and I went as Cooperman, a Russ Abbot character based on Superman. By the end of the night I was in a right state and went in search of a taxi home. It was the usual situation where you can't get a cab at Christmas because everyone is out celebrating.

Finally I managed to flag one down and said: "Woolton please." The driver looked me up and down and said: "I'm not going anywhere. If you're Cooperman you can fly home." And off he drove. I'm sure he was an Evertonian. I had to ring my missus for a lift instead.

Even now the Liverpool lads still get dressed up for the Christmas night out. Steven Gerrard's disguise as an old man in a mobility scooter a few years ago was brilliant.

When they had one of the get-togethers in my bar in town I went along, although Robbie Fowler probably wished I hadn't. There was karaoke and quite a few drinks, and at the end of the evening the lads had agreed to draw out a name to decide who would pay the bar bill.

They asked me to do the honours and it was Robbie's name I pulled from the tombola. He was absolutely gutted and really annoyed with me. The bill would have been a few grand. "You own streets in Manchester, you can afford it" I joked, referring to the fact that he has bought a lot of property, and we all had a laugh about it.

Even when it wasn't the festive season we were always up for a few pints at Anfield. Usually we'd head straight to the players' lounge after a game.

Some of the lads who had been around for a while even had their own spots at the bar, such as Alan Hansen. I didn't know that and neither did my dad when he came to watch one of my first games for the club.

I'd arranged to meet him in the lounge afterwards and when I got there he was standing in Jockey's spot. "You're in my place," Alan told him. "It's not your place now," my old man responded as he refused to move.

Usually Steve Nicol was first to the bar at Anfield and I was not far behind him. All the ale was free, so it was great. Then we'd make our way into town. There was always a group of us. Lads like Ray Houghton and Steve McMahon would often be there and Gary Ablett too, although he didn't always go out. Gary Gillespie, or me if I'm honest, were probably the worst when it came to getting a round in.

In town we had a few regular haunts, such as Tommy Smith's bar. That was the venue where Mike Hooper went for a new personal record. Mike's a big lad and he could put a fair bit away. He lined up eight pints and one of his mates readied the stopwatch. Mike sunk all the pints in about 35 seconds. I've never seen anything like it.

If we'd played on a Saturday I'd go to Garston the following afternoon. There I'd have a pint with my dad until 3pm, then go home for my Sunday dinner and a sleep before heading back out again that night.

Monday morning meant we'd usually train and work off the alcohol from the weekend. That was difficult some days. But it never affected anyone's game because we were professionals. If we were playing on a Tuesday night we wouldn't go out the Sunday before, we'd never be that stupid. Drinking so close to a game was never something I did too often, even if a few pints the night before a match once helped me score a hat-trick for Oxford. I'd unexpectedly ended up going out with my dad and drank a few beers. The next day I scored three in a 4-2 win over Luton. Despite that success it wasn't something I practiced. It would have led to far too much trouble.

The only time I remember anyone complaining about nights out at Liverpool was when Kenny called in Ray Houghton and I after training one day and said we'd been drinking too much.

On the other side of Stanley Park Everton also adopted the same approach. If they'd lost they would go out on a Wednesday and have a few beers. At first it worked, the results always came good again after a get together. Then suddenly they suffered a defeat after a day out together and Howard Kendall had a rethink.

He came in the next day and said: "Right lads, we're not going out on a Wednesday anymore... We'll be going out on a Tuesday instead."

Drinking took place throughout the year, but we'd really go for it when there was no serious football to be played. Post-season tours were a great excuse for a few beers. In 1987 we travelled to the Middle East for a friendly with Israel. Despite arriving there early in the morning we didn't go to bed.

Instead, beer and breakfast was on the menu, followed by a day out. Eventually, wearily, we made our way to the hotel quite a few hours later. A training session the next day wasn't what any of us required, especially Steve McMahon, who left the contents of his stomach on the team bus afterwards.

At the end of the same summer we were on it again during our pre-season tour. Barry Venison ended up having to foot the bill for £170 worth of champagne. Thankfully none of us had to look after the tab when we went to the PFA Awards in London because the price was ridiculous. Despite five of us being on the Team of the Season they positioned us near the door.

Rightly, we felt we should have been on a better table and were thinking about leaving. The PFA Chief Gordon Taylor knew we were unhappy and tried to solve the problem. He did, by offering for the FA to cover the cost of our drinks.

I'm sure he regretted it afterwards as we consumed a load of Bollinger champagne. It didn't do us any harm, though. Three days later we went out and beat Forest 5-0 at Anfield.

LOCKED UP

Usually our drinking was harmless, a way to enjoy ourselves and get away from the pressures that came with being professional footballers. Or at least that was the intention when Joan and I went out with Ray Houghton and his missus following a 0-0 draw with Norwich City.

After a few beers we went to a nightclub where I got in an argument with a barwoman. The drinks had clearly taken their toll on me and I was silly because I should have known there would be trouble when the bouncers got involved. They were deliberately trying to wind me up and I took the bait.

I reacted the way they wanted me to and, before I knew it, they were throwing me down some steps. On the street the police were nearby and I started to tell them about how I'd been treated, or assaulted.

As I did one of the bouncers came out and I went for him. I completely lost the plot, right in front of the cops. Any sympathy they may have had for me was quickly wiped out and they had little choice but to arrest me. I spent a few hours in a cell and it's something I completely regret now. The police were fine about it but when they have to get involved it's not good. I was later cleared of the charges in court.

When I had the bust-up with Kenny near the end of my Liverpool career he said that I shit on the club.

I assume getting arrested is what he meant. I think that was unfair. I did the wrong thing and I knew that. Jan Molby was put in jail for a few months and they welcomed him back with open arms. I should have been forgiven too.

IRISH SPIRIT

If the cops in Liverpool sometimes had to end my nights out the Irish police, or Garda Siochana, usually helped us start the evening in Ireland.

On many occasions after games, they would give us an escort into town. They'd let the bus driver have a few pints and then drive us home too. Now and again the police who were accompanying us would have a few drinks in the bar or back at the hotel too.

It was like one big family with everyone having a good time. I don't think it could happen to the same extent now. There is too much media coverage and people with camera phones everywhere. If players did the same things they'd be in the papers all the time.

It was never a problem under Jack Charlton. He'd let us drink before games and wouldn't run us too hard in training. He wanted us to keep all our energy for the match.

As far as I was concerned that was good psychology because when the game came along you wanted to run the beer off and were also bursting to get out on the pitch. It obviously worked.

I know that Giovanni Trapattoni lets the lads have a few drinks and unwind now, although it can't be to the same extent as we did.

After Ireland played Algeria at the end of the 2009/10 season I was over in Dublin for the game. I went out in Swords, a town just outside Dublin, with Jason that night and a few of the players were there too.

We had a chat and they told us Trapattoni lets them relax when the time is right. The players have so much respect for him and rightly so.

CHANGING MY WAYS IN SPAIN

As I pulled an oxygen mask over my face I knew my previous drinking habits at Newport, Oxford and Liverpool would have to change.

I hadn't even kicked a ball for Sociedad, but the rigorous nature of the medical convinced me I wouldn't be able to go for a few beers after the game any more. It was as tough as any pre-season training session and I remember being completely drained after spending so much time pedalling on an exercise bike. The doctors carried out a load of tests to see if I was lacking in vitamins or minerals. The medical set-up was far more advanced than anything else I had experienced. Re-hydration was a major priority. My previous way of re-hydrating had been to down ten pints.

It wasn't just fluids either, everything we needed to eat was worked out exactly right. It made the dietary set-up back at Liverpool look antiquated.

In my time at Anfield we'd eaten what we liked. I usually had a Scotch pie and beans on the Friday before a game. If we had a Saturday fixture we'd go to The Moathouse Hotel and have chicken and beans, or maybe steak. If it were steak it would be huge, maybe weighing a pound and the chicken would be half of a full bird sliced down the middle. Then, for dessert, we'd sometimes have rice pudding too.

After eating all that I was never sure how I'd start a game. Sometimes I'd feel full of energy, other days I'd be really lethargic. There was no logic to it. In Spain it was all measured to perfection to ensure you were just right. I adjusted to it, I'm not sure some of my former team-mates would have.

Steve Nicol in particular would have really struggled. 'Chips' we used to call him because he'd eat so much. I roomed with him once and the amount of food he consumed was absolutely frightening.

In the room he ate club sandwiches before going downstairs and having a huge feed for dinner. Later that same

ALRIGHT ALDO

night he was munching crisps before he started sleepwalking.
I couldn't believe it and always tried to have a different
roommate from then on!

Playing on a Sunday every week in Spain also meant a big
change for me. Back in England that was usually my day for
a few drinks. Instead I'd go out with the missus and have
some food and wine after the match.

It was only when Dalian Atkinson and Kevin Richardson
arrived at Sociedad that I had regular drinking partners.
Naturally we took it too far now and again, especially one
Thursday night when a friend of mine invited us to a local
society. We ate and drank like kings before going for a few
more beers in the town. The next day at training wasn't fun
and we couldn't fool the manager. He fined us £1,000 each.

Apart from us three the other players just weren't into
nights out and usually went home early. There was only a
handful of occasions when they stayed out late; even then
they went home at 2am so it wasn't an all-nighter. That way
of living might not have seemed as much fun but I think it's
one of the reasons why I played until I was nearly 40.

TRANMERE – AND A PRE-MATCH MASSAGE
Having slightly altered my social habits in Spain meant I found
the routine at Tranmere unusual at first. We regularly played
at Prenton Park on a Friday night. It meant we could go on the
beer for the rest of the weekend.

Away games normally involved a few beers the evening
before. We'd drink from about half nine until closing time. I'd
have a couple of glasses of wine while others, like Eric Nixon
and Kenny Irons, would sometimes have about six pints. And
they might bring cans back to the hotel too. It never affected
our performance the following day, even if it wasn't ideal pre-
match preparation.

Drinking wasn't the only unusual way of getting ready for a
game at Tranmere. During my first season some of the
younger lads had a different way of 'preparing'. Before one

game Johnny King told us to go for a walk. We had only gone a short way down the road when we passed a massage parlour. After the pre-match lunch a few of the lads went for another walk, straight to the massage parlour. On their return there was a squelching sound whenever they moved. Apparently the massage oil had dripped into their shoes. We won 2-1 at Derby County so it must have been a great massage.

That wasn't a tradition I encouraged when I became manager. One I did start, and tried to maintain, was a squad night out if results were going against us. I'd picked that up from my time at Anfield where it had been a routine since the days of Bill Shankly. We'd go into Liverpool and have a meal and maybe visit a lap-dancing club. Everyone had to turn up, that was the only rule. It took the pressure off the lads and helped them relax.

DRESSING ROOM BANTER

"Woof, woof," a few of us would bark. "That's my food for today, that's for tomorrow and that's for the following day. I won't eat it all in one go," someone would say as everyone else laughed loudly.

The comments began after a story about Roy Keane reached the Ireland dressing room. Apparently when Roy was living on his own he had a Labrador dog. He was going to Dublin for a few days for a game and before he went to the airport he laid out the dog's food for each of the days he'd be away. When he got back the dog was dead. Of course, it had eaten all the food in one sitting and died because of it.

"Please don't tell him I told you," Denis Irwin said as he passed on the story and tried to stop laughing. We all got great amusement from it.

Humour like that showed there was a good spirit in the group and we all got on. That came from socialising together whenever the team met up. Because we knew each other well we could take the piss a lot. I always had banter with Roy about Liverpool and Manchester United; even if he could be quiet a lot of the time.

On the pitch he was a dream to play with, an absolutely brilliant player. Roy wouldn't say much but Denis would always pass on funny stories about what was happening at United.

Another featuring Roy involved him buying a brand new watch. He paid for it on his card and thought he'd got a bargain as it cost only £1,200. Apparently he was pretty pleased with himself as he showed Denis, who quickly pointed out it had cost £12,000 not £1,200. Roy was fuming.

In the Ireland dressing room there were loads of jokers, with Andy Townsend and Ronnie Whelan probably being the biggest of the lot. They were always messing around, looking to have a bit of fun – usually at somebody's expense, though nobody minded.

That ability to laugh at ourselves definitely helped us become successful. On international duty at World Cups and the European Championships it was particularly important because you spent an awful lot of time away from home and hanging around the hotel. You needed light-hearted moments and good company to alleviate the boredom in between training sessions and the match coming around.

At Liverpool everyone was capable of chipping in with a good line too, lads like Steve McMahon and Steve Nicol were always some of the first to do so.

When I look at football now I don't think it can be the same. There are players from all over the world, many who speak different languages and come from different cultures.

I'm not saying that it's impossible for a team like that to bond. After all, you only have to look at the results on the pitch to see that those teams can be successful. But I still think that it's more difficult to have the same spirit and togetherness that we enjoyed.

TEAM SPIRIT – MY FAVOURITE DRINKS

1. Red wine

2. Tetley's Smooth Flow

3. Cristal Pilsener (Portugal)

4. San Miguel

5. Tea

6. Coffee

7. Guinness

8. Water

EIGHT DRESSING ROOM JOKERS

1. Ronnie Whelan

2. John Sheridan

3. Andy Townsend

4. Steve McMahon

5. Dalian Atkinson

6. Johnny Morrissey

7. The entire Tranmere Rovers squad

8. Steve Nicol

EIGHT LIVERPOOL PLAYERS' FANCY DRESS OUTFITS

1. Cooperman – me

2. A pensioner – Steven Gerrard

3. Ku Klux Klan – John Barnes

4. The Mad Hatter – Stan (Steve Staunton)

5. A judge – Kenny Dalglish

6. A Beefeater – Ian Rush

7. The Joker – Bruce Grobbelaar

8. Dick Turpin – Barnesie again

£

SOUND AS A POUND

'John Aldridge today called on Liverpool fans worldwide to join him in an audacious attempt to buy the club. The Reds legend has pledged £5,000 to buy a share in the ambitious Share Liverpool scheme.

'He said: "As someone who was fortunate enough to play for the club and who loves the club dearly, it hurts me to see it in the kind of turmoil it has been in recently. I've pledged and I would call on all Liverpool supporters around the world to do the same.

"If we get together and buy the club outright it would be a dream come true..."'

– Liverpool Echo, 2007

My ShareLiverpoolFC certificate
and my usual bet – banking on
Stevie to deliver the goods...

THE DAY BILL SHOWED HE CARES

"Fuck off John," Bill Kenwright said loudly as he shook my hand and gave me a hug.

Some people haven't got time for the Everton Chairman. He went up a lot in my opinion on the day Tranmere knocked his team out of the FA Cup at Goodison Park.

Naturally I'd been thrilled by my team's 3-0 win in January, 2001, and the comprehensive nature of it. We hadn't just eliminated them, we had humiliated them.

Most of those connected with the Blues congratulated me and shook my hand in the board room afterwards. Sir Philip Carter was a true gentleman. He made a point of congratulating me warmly, which I thought summed up what a great man he is. Then I spotted Bill walking towards me.

I wasn't sure what kind of a reaction I was going to get from him. What I did receive were honest words that we both laughed about. I thought his reaction was great because it showed exactly how he felt. If your team had just been battered at home in the FA Cup by a lower league side you are going to be pissed off, and he didn't try to hide that fact. He cares about the club and that is great to see.

Unfortunately on the other side of Stanley Park the attitude of some owners in recent years has been about as far removed from Kenwright's as Merseyside is from America. Tom Hicks and George Gillett – or Stadler and Waldorf from the Muppet Show – never really cared about Liverpool.

I was at Anfield during one of their first visits. Steve Hothersall was interviewing them for City and I was in the background just listening. I wasn't sure about their intentions at that time but I never thought they'd mess things up so badly. Share Liverpool, the organisation that wants to buy the club and model it on Barcelona, said that with the Yanks in charge there was only one way we could go and that was down. During 2009/10, their premonition came true.

'YOU'LL PLAY FOR ENGLAND ONE DAY' – MAXWELL

The Yanks who took over Liverpool failed to provide the money they promised at Liverpool. That was never the case with Robert Maxwell when I played for Oxford United.

His biggest fault when it came to football was his naivety. People laughed at his expense because he didn't know anything about the game. He bizarrely said I could play for England one day, even though I had already featured for Ireland.

During the negotiation of my transfer to Liverpool he phoned chairman John Smith and said while I was in the room that I should be on the same money as Rushie. He knew how much I wanted to make the move but insisted I stay until Oxford were out of the FA Cup. That really annoyed me and delayed my switch back home. Looking at it rationally I can see that he was trying to look after his team.

MONEY'S TOO TIGHT TO MENTION

When I first took charge as manager of Tranmere, I was told we were losing £1.7m a year. During my reign we brought in plenty of revenue, in total it was roughly £15m. That came from selling players and the TV money we received for the big cup games. The best example of just how bad, and bizarre, our finances were came in 2001.

The unforgettable win over Southampton after being 3-0 down at half-time had sent us through to the quarter-finals of the FA Cup, and a home tie with Liverpool. The whole country wanted to see if we could do it again. The TV companies stumped up a lot of cash and all the tickets sold out. Money was undoubtedly rolling in, but again the club couldn't afford to give me anything to strengthen the squad.

I laugh when I hear managers now talking about not having money to spend. The only players I ever bought for any decent sums were Wayne Allison for a couple of hundred thousand and David Kelly. Usually I had to sign lads like Andy Thorn, Paul Rideout and Stuart Barlow who were coming near the end of their careers. They did a fantastic job for me, but because of their age it was only ever going to be on a short-term basis. Stuart was a great fella who never stopped talking. I was always afraid to let him into my office. Once he got in he'd stay there and I wouldn't get a word in.

Older pros replacing youngsters means there is no continuity. You have to keep bringing in players as the older lads retire or move on again. You can't plan for the long term because you know in a year, or six months, two or three positions will need to be filled again.

I tried to find answers to the money problems at Rovers on numerous occasions. The money situation had been bothering me for a while and on the way home from a game at Nottingham Forest, it was really on my mind.

I'd had to use a lot of the younger players on the day, against a side who were top of the league. I'd even had to give them a few pints of Guinness the night before to settle their nerves.

They performed brilliantly to help earn us a point. But I knew we couldn't keep turning to them. We needed to buy new players with experience. After chatting to one of the directors, he suggested we confront the chairman at a board meeting the following week. I thought this sounded like a good idea and we were finally going to get an answer.

During the meeting we eventually got to the manager's report. It usually contained news on injuries and suspensions – Kenny Irons being banned for swearing at the ref again – that sort of thing.

We went through it and then I said to Frank Corfe: "Chairman, it's irrelevant. We're losing £1.7m a year and we have to sell all our best players to survive. We need money to strengthen the squad. When is that going to happen?"

I then waited for someone else to say something. Nobody stood up in support of what I had said... despite that director promising to back me up (he knows who he is). The whole episode hurt me. In the end I felt I couldn't really trust certain people behind the scenes at Tranmere. That was part of the reason why I left.

COUGHING UP TO BUY NEW PLAYERS

Even though I did leave, nobody could question how much I cared about Tranmere Rovers. I even delved into my own pocket to keep them in business. On more than one occasion bankruptcy looked a certainty. The administrators were coming in and it got so bad that chairman Lorraine Rogers told me we needed to sell more players quickly.

I was going away to Portugal for a holiday with my wife when Lorraine asked if I could lend the club any money. She said £50,000 would keep the administrators away for a month while some sales were made to raise cash. I got my cheque book out. Lorraine assured me I'd get the cash back. She also said if we did sell anyone I'd get five per cent of the fee. I wasn't in it for that but I wasn't going to say no either. I was still away and she rang to say Huddersfield had come in with an offer of £500,000 for Kenny Irons. A cheque eventually came through to me for the five per cent, all taxed and above board. Then when John McGreal was sold to Ipswich she gave me my £50,000 back. There was no five per cent on top of that. It didn't matter to me because we had staved off the administrators.

My generosity was conveniently forgotten when it came to my final pay cheque from the club. I'd left halfway through March, 2001, and they only paid me up until that date. They didn't even have the respect to give me a full month's pay.

I'd given them nearly ten years of my life and taken them to their first ever major cup final. That was how they rewarded me. That told me I'd made the right choice by leaving. I didn't want the cash; I'd rather it was given to charity. It's the principle of the matter. That was a disappointing way to behave.

£78 A WEEK

If my last payslip in professional football was sickening, my first didn't impress me either. It was £78 per week; I'd been on £82 as a toolmaker just prior to that. Because I was a mate of Robin Ashurst, his brother Len knew how much I was making and offered me £4 less to play for Newport County back in 1978. On top of that there was a £10 appearance bonus and £20 for every point the team picked up.

Modern players don't have to rely on bonuses, the thought of that extra cash was brilliant motivation for me to work harder in training and play better. And as I progressed up through football's different levels my wages rose accordingly, except for when it came to the international stage.

At a time when England players were on roughly £1,000 per game, at Ireland we got 125 punts for a friendly and 250 punts for a competitive match. It showed the press didn't have an idea what they were talking about when they referred to us as mercenaries who played just for the money. Their comments just spurred us on to do our country proud.

VORONIN ON £47,000 A WEEK?

I remember being in America with Ireland in the early Nineties when me and Andy Townsend were reading about the wages the basketball players were on, people like Michael Jordan. We couldn't believe the figures involved and we agreed football would never go that way. Now it has.

You don't mind top players like Gerrard, Torres, Rooney and Ronaldo getting the top wages. They deserve it because they bring a lot of cash into the game. It's when you see the likes of former Liverpool player Andriy Voronin – he was reportedly on £47,000 per week – it becomes disgusting. Some players just aren't good enough but they are on a couple of million quid a year. There has to be a capping system put in place before everything goes bust. Maybe players can earn on top of their wages through images rights instead.

Having awful players on big cash takes the game further and further away from normal people. You have guys who graft all week to barely make enough to take their kids to the match. When they do manage to go, there are these professionals playing who appear like they don't care. Seeing that attitude hurts me. As well as being paid big wages plenty of these average players move around all the time, therefore bringing in more money in signing on fees.

THE LEAVING OF LIVERPOOL

£15,000 was what Liverpool were willing to pay me to join Real Sociedad in 1989. "Piss off," I told a shocked Peter Robinson, the former club secretary, when I heard this. Unlike some players, I wasn't always being transferred to rake in the cash through different pay-offs and signing on fees.

At the same time, I wasn't going to be treated like an idiot as I felt, rightly or wrongly, that I was getting forced out of the club I loved. My argument was they were going to make £400,000 profit out of the deal and were only giving me a tiny percentage of that figure. Robinson countered with the point that I could have been rubbish when they took the chance on an Oxford United striker. I was quick to respond with my goalscoring record – 63 in 104 appearances for Liverpool – figures that proved I'd done well. £250,000 was what I told them I wanted, even though I never expected to receive it.

Eventually, after a chat with Dennis Roach, an agent who brokered the deal for the two clubs, they offered me a different but acceptable sum. I said "Hello" to Robinson when I went back to Anfield a few years later and felt he ignored me. We haven't spoken since. Perhaps he was embarrassed because I showed him up in front of the chairman.

MY ONE DAY AS A FOOTBALL AGENT

When I came back to England from Spain I had a phone call from the Special Branch. They wanted a chat about the finer details of my move from Liverpool to Sociedad.

The suggestion was that some organisation or other had made cash from the deal. These investigators asked if I could help them. I didn't know anything about the company or who they were, and the investigation ended there. Incidents like that are the reason why I could never be a football agent. Andy Townsend once asked me if I'd be interested in setting up an agency with him. I didn't want to get involved because I've seen how the majority of them operate. I've also given it a try so I'm speaking from experience.

My one day as a negotiator could have resulted in Dalian Atkinson moving to Atletico Madrid to team up with Paolo Futre. Dalian had caught the eye of the Spanish club with some great performances for Sociedad.

They wanted to talk to him about the possibility of a transfer and Dalian asked if I'd help him do the deal. He didn't want his agent Dennis Roach involved.

We also demanded a translator be present, even though my Spanish was pretty good by then. Atletico asked how much Dalian wanted.

He said: "What's Futre on?" He was their best player, and was earning around £11,000 net of tax a week. That was a huge amount back then. The Atletico representatives said they couldn't afford to pay that much.

We did agree on a decent sum and they also offered a house. Dalian decided to be cheeky and asked for a Ferrari Testarossa. Not only that, he wanted one in Spain and one in England. Unsurprisingly we never heard from them again after that suggestion.

SPANISH PROPOSITION

Like Dalian I never got £11,000 per week. But I did make good money from football, all of it honest. There were opportunities to earn a little more on the side too, through other means such as when Sociedad faced RDC Mallorca in my last Spanish league outing.

A win for us would have kept Espanol in the division. During the build-up to the game, someone from Barcelona's other club got in contact with one of my colleagues and suggested there would be a bonus for us if we got a victory. It amounted to £4,000 each.

Naturally we all refused and didn't want anything to do with it. But the game still contained some suspicious moments that made me wonder if some bribery had taken place. On more than one occasion I was definitely fouled in the box. The ref didn't give any penalty and it finished 0-0. Mallorca were saved and Espanol avoided the drop too.

The truth was I didn't need to earn extra money through dishonest means. I was already well rewarded. The money I made from the game I invested wisely. That's why my family are comfortable now.

I'm not envious when I hear about how much Premier League players take in. Their wages are eye-popping but I think we had a better lifestyle.

We could go out for a pint together and never usually be hassled by anyone. Some of the most famous footballers can't even go outside their own front door now which must drive them mad at times.

JACK TAKES IT TO HEART

As well as making money football can also help you to lose it just as quickly.

With most teams I played for, cards was usually how we killed time and squandered some of our earnings. The Irish squad had a very competitive card school; on one occasion it even cost Kevin Sheedy his place in the team!

Hearts was our usual game and 'Sheeds' dealt Jack Charlton a bad hand, which resulted in him losing a few quid. Jack was raging and left him out of the side for our game, though being serious, I'm sure this wasn't the main reason.

Nearly every member of our squad could play to some standard. Kevin Moran was good, Tony Cascarino is a professional gambler now, Quinny, Paul McGrath, John Sheridan and Denis Irwin got involved too.

At Euro '88 I lost a load of money, a couple of grand. Because we'd had such a great time at the end of the tournament Liam Brady said the lads wouldn't take the cash from me. That summed up how close the group was.

Sometimes I didn't even mind losing, such as the day I discovered Liverpool wanted to buy me from Oxford. On the way back from our match at Manchester City the bus had a few engine problems.

To pass the time the cards were brought out. In an hour and a half I lost a week's wages to Billy Whitehurst, Kevin Brock and Les Phillips. Even taking such a hit couldn't extinguish my happiness because I knew I was going to Anfield.

Betting was another way to lose money quickly. Thankfully I never got involved too much even though I do like a flutter. I usually go for Steven Gerrard to score first or last when Liverpool play at home.

If I don't do it he is nearly guaranteed to score the opening or closing goal.

I've also been at the centre of some big gambling wins; unfortunately the money didn't come my way. At Oxford an unknown gambler put £8,000 on us winning the Second Division. We did and, at odds of 16-1, it turned out to be the club owner Robert Maxwell who picked up a nice wad of cash.

A few years later, during my first season at Tranmere, a director by the name of Fred Williams placed £1,000 on me reaching 40 goals in all competitions.

The odds were 25/1 and I achieved it with a goal in our 2-1 defeat against Oxford on the last day of the season.

Most of the cash rightly went to charity, with Fred using a small percentage of it to fund a cracking night out for the players.

£500 - ANYBODY IN?

ALDO CALLS ON FANS TO HELP BUY CLUB
– Headline in the Liverpool Echo, March 2007

I may have paid from my own pocket to help Tranmere as a manager but over recent years I have happily handed over more money to try and buy a club – Liverpool Football Club.

No, I haven't suddenly come in to big money and I can't afford to buy the club on my own but I was giving my support to a scheme called 'Share Liverpool', set up by University of Liverpool academic and lifelong Liverpudlian Rogan Taylor.

The idea, put very simply, is that fans contribute some of their own money and we all buy the club – our club. It might sound ridiculous but it could work. I honestly believe it can become a reality as long as the fans believe in it.

As someone who was fortunate enough to play for the club and who loves Liverpool FC dearly, it hurts me to see it in the kind of turmoil it has been in recently. That's why when Rogan told me about his plan I thought it was a fantastic idea. Phil Thompson agreed and gave his support to the scheme too, right from the start. It's all about putting power in the hands of the fans and that could only be a good thing.

I pledged an initial sum of £5000 and I would call on all Liverpool supporters around the world to pledge too. I know £500 (the cost of a share was later reduced) is not an insignificant amount of money but the beauty of Share Liverpool is groups of fans can get together to buy a share between them, you don't have to be rich to buy one.

If we get together and buy the club outright it would be a dream come true. It would put the power in the hands of the people who love Liverpool most and it would also make the club incredibly powerful because there would be no profits or share dividends going elsewhere. Every penny generated would go back into the club. How many other teams in Europe could boast that kind of spending power?

Having played in Spain, I have witnessed at close quarters how the Barcelona model helps make the Catalan giants one of the most powerful clubs in Spain and beyond.

Ok, there is one important difference. Barcelona fans haven't had to fork out millions of pounds between them. But when you look at what a fantastic club Barca is, it should inspire everyone who loves Liverpool to at least try and do something similar. It can't be a coincidence that Barcelona are always in the running for the biggest prizes. That comes down to the way the club is run, from the members upwards.

Like Barcelona, Liverpool is a special club and I've no doubt our fan base is big enough to get the number we need. We are one of the best supported clubs in the world, up there with the likes of Man United, Barcelona and AC Milan. When you have such strength anything is possible. Even with new owners coming in, they could give 10 per cent of the club back to the fans and they could still own a significant stake.

INDEPENDENCE DAY

As Liverpool fans, we have to stand up for what we feel is right. That's what makes us different from other clubs. That's why I was happy to take part in the 'Our Independence Day' rally on July 4, 2010.

It took part at St George's Hall in Liverpool city centre and was well supported with a crowd of between 2,000 and 5,000 turning up. It was organised by the Spirit of Shankly group to protest against the owners and to call for change in the boardroom. I addressed the crowd and spoke on behalf of Share Liverpool.

It's easy to sit back, watch the telly and do nothing about the problems behind the scenes or you can try and do things that may help along the way. That's all I'm trying to do. Whether it makes any difference or not, at least I've tried, along with other people within their city who have got off their arses. The people who mock or deride us are sitting back doing nothing.

MY CAREER IN MONEY

(Some figures may not be spot on but it gives you an idea)
£82 per week as a toolmaker
£78 per week basic at Newport County
£1.15m (fee from Liverpool to Real Sociedad)
£350 per week at Oxford United
100,000 punts (cash raised by Irish fans after USA '94 fine)
125 punts per friendly for Ireland
250 punts per competitive game for Ireland
£2.7m to bring Rushie back to Anfield (I remember it well!)

EIGHT PLAYERS TRANMERE COULDN'T KEEP BECAUSE OF FINANCIAL PROBLEMS

1. Ian Moore to Nottingham Forest £1m
2. Alan Rogers to Nottingham Forest £2m
3. Ged Brannan to Man City £750,000
4. Steve Simonsen to Everton*
5. Kenny Irons to Huddersfield £500,000
6. John McGreal to Ipswich £650,000
7. Alan Mahon to Sporting Lisbon free (they later sold him to Blackburn for £1.5m)
8. Ivano Bonetti (if he had stayed I would have been fined a fortune by the powers that be for what I did to him!)
* Who knows what the final figure was, some say £3.3m.

EIGHT BIG MONEY LIVERPOOL PLAYERS

(Good and bad, in no particular order)
1. Kenny Dalglish
2. Stan Collymore
3. Fernando Torres
4. Djibril Cisse
5. Dean Saunders
6. John Barnes
7. Alun Evans
8. Ryan Babel

124

SPANISH RED

'John Aldridge yesterday earned 40 bottles of wine and 20 kilos of Spanish sausages after he scored twice in the 4-1 win over Rayo Vallecano to become the first Real Sociedad player to score in six consecutive league matches'

– *Daily Mirror, March 1990*

Bits and pieces – I.D cards and documentation
I have kept from my time in Spain...

'NO OUTSIDERS'

Before the arrival of Sky the Welsh TV channel S4C was the best place to watch Spanish football in the UK. Because of that, and former Liverpool player John Toshack's spell there as manager, I was aware of Real Sociedad, even if I didn't know a lot about the club.

It was obvious that, although certain people at Anfield wanted me out back in 1989, they weren't going to let me join Arsenal or another of the country's top sides. I didn't want to either, so when the opportunity to go to San Sebastian arose I immediately fancied it.

I spoke with Joan and she was scared about moving abroad. The kids were young too. We weighed up the options. The money Sociedad offered me was phenomenal. I was getting roughly five times what I had been on at Liverpool. Over the three years of my contract it would be enough to guarantee us a decent future. It really was too good to turn down.

I told Joan that if she didn't like it she could move back home and travel out to see me every few weeks. I just wanted her to give it a try. On the Thursday after Liverpool battered Palace 9-0 we flew to Spain for my unveiling. The financial benefits didn't ease the process of going straight into what was a politically delicate situation. A lot of people simply didn't want me there. And a few protestors turned up outside the hotel where we were meeting the club officials.

I sat with the interpreter. There was loads of media interest and the journalists wanted to know how I was going to handle the situation.

I told them: "I was very proud to be joining such a great club as Real Sociedad. I was here to play football and score goals. I don't care about anything else that goes with it. I know I'm the first non-Basque to join in a long time but give me a chance to show what I can do."

That was exactly what John Toshack had told me to say so I knew those were wise words. Even that wasn't enough for some people though.

'No outsiders' was scrawled on the walls at the training ground in Spanish. I didn't know what it meant at the time. Someone spat on the floor in front of me in the street. And even in my first game against Osasuna, a 1-0 win in a poor match, I could tell a lot of the supporters were still unsure about me.

Some sang my name, others completely ignored me. Then a few weeks later I got both goals in a 2-2 draw with Barcelona at home.

After that I noticed people's attitudes towards me altered. I didn't mind their original stance because, wherever you go in the world, people are going to have a different way of living or thinking. That was how it worked at Sociedad and I had to get on with it. Over time it became easier and people's stance changed.

A NEW COUNTRY, A NEW GAME

Change was something I had to focus on myself as I tried to adjust to a completely different type of football compared to what I'd grown up with.

The Spanish way of playing was a lot more tactical and technical.

Around that time the English First Division was really a blood and thunder type of game. La Liga was different, on occasions I wouldn't even get a kick away from home. As I've mentioned elsewhere, it was hugely frustrating at times. It took me a few weeks to adjust to what was a tough league to score goals in.

Once I did, I always did okay in a side that wasn't over generous when it came to creating chances. I never lost any confidence in myself because I always believed I'd do my job. I would have liked to go to play in Italy too, I'm sure I'd have found the net plenty of times there also.

At Sociedad we struggled in my second year, but I still managed to do okay. If I could do it there I could have done it in any other country.

LEARNING US TO TALK LIKE 'EM

I'd hated school, and really hated learning French. Attempting to pick up the language of my new homeland wasn't a problem though. I actually relished the idea.

After training my tutor would come to the villa and we'd sit down for an hour working on the basics. Then on a Monday I'd go to Robinsons Bar by the ground and have a few drinks. I wasn't allowed to talk English with the other people present unless I was asking what something meant.

I also picked up plenty of the language just by being around my team-mates; unfortunately it was usually swear words they passed on.

People in Spain don't swear anywhere near as much as we do in this country. It's as if we have Tourettes Syndrome over here. I'd make up my own swear words over there by combining different words. The lads in the dressing room loved it.

Every day they'd be asking me what I'd come up with. I'd tell them what it was in English first and then give them my rough version of a Spanish translation. It probably didn't make any sense but helped me to practice and get to know the rest of the squad.

It meant that by the time Dalian Atkinson and Kevin Richardson arrived at the club later I'd settled in well and was able to help them out. We had some great times together. Dalian and I would go to Kevin's house where he'd be drinking vodka and tonic, pints of it.

The lifestyle off the field was a lot more relaxed than what I'd been used to. Fans would let you go about your business and barely pay you any attention. They were friendly people, a fact that was emphasised to me when Joan's brothers were staying with us. We went for a few beers in my local, with only a few people in there.

By the time 1am came around we were still drinking, and also starving. I asked the guy behind the bar if he was serving food, fully expecting a negative response.

He said yes and asked what we wanted. "Four steak and chips," I said. He nodded his head and disappeared upstairs. Then, down the stairs with her dressing gown on, came his wife. He'd woken her up to cook our dinner.

We felt terrible about it. The food tasted great though. That night was an example of how the locals couldn't do enough for you. San Sebastian is a wonderful city and one of the gourmet capitals of Europe. I enjoyed some of the best food and wine that I've ever tasted there.

A SURPRISE RETURN TO ANFIELD

August 14, 1990. Liverpool vs Real Sociedad, Kenny Dalglish's testimonial...

When I heard Kenny wanted my new side to travel to Anfield for his testimonial I was surprised. He could have had any team in the world to take part in the game, Celtic being the one most people would have expected him to go for. Instead he picked Sociedad.

You'll have to ask him why he chose that particular opposition. Whatever the reasons for it I didn't care, it was great to come back and play in front of the Kop. I loved it, and so did my team-mates. The Sociedad lads thought the stadium and the fans were unbelievable. They talked about it for ages afterwards.

Years later I discussed how special the ground is with Xabi Alonso at the Liverpool players' Christmas party. Some of his mates were over with him and we talked about how good the Basque region is. It was a place I wouldn't have left if my family hadn't become unsettled after two seasons. That was the most important factor for me. And what ultimately made my mind up.

I wish I could have stayed in Spain to see out my contract. I felt I owed the club something because they had been good to me. John Toshack, who had been Sociedad boss before moving on to Real Madrid, had returned to take over from Marco Boronat as manager. He wanted me to stay too.

I couldn't, I had to put my family first. Because of that I didn't leave on good terms. The president, Luis Arconada, believed I should stay and was refusing to agree to what I wanted. As we put forward both sides of the argument it looked like a fight would ensue.

The dispute continued until the start of the new campaign. My switch to Tranmere – and more importantly our move back to Merseyside – was in doubt even as the season kicked off.

Thankfully John Toshack helped to smooth things over and I was able to become a Rover. The style of my departure from Sociedad was sour. But my affection for the people and the place remains to this day.

They were promoted back to the Premier Division at the end of the 2009/10 season and I was delighted to see that. Hopefully I can travel over to watch them in action soon.

It will also give me a chance to brush up on my rusty Spanish...

XABI WHO?

My Spanish would have came in very useful the first time I met Xabi Alonso, had I recognised him that is. I have to hold my hand up and say I didn't have a clue who Xabi was when I bumped into him at Anfield.

If you remember, the season had already started before Xabi pulled on a red shirt for the first time. I was working at a game in August, 2004, when someone with a Spanish accent stopped me on the stairs for a chat. "Who is this?" I remember thinking to myself as he continued to talk to me.

When I walked away I'd only gone a few steps down before it dawned on me. Xabi had recognised me because he grew up supporting Sociedad. I should have known it was him as I'd watched him play on TV loads of times.

Straight away I ran back, gave him my number and told him to buzz me if he ever needed anything.

RAFA'S REIGN

Between the summers of 2004 and 2010 Spanish seemed to be the language you required if you were going to make it at Liverpool. I don't think I ever encountered Rafa Benitez during my time in Spain. What I did know about him was the fact he'd done well with Valencia.

At the time of his arrival in England I was still pissed off with Gerard Houllier and the type of players he had brought in. The type of football being played under him was horrendous. I hated watching it. In my opinion, Phil Thompson got the team playing better in the time he was in charge. The players seemed to give more when Thommo was the boss. If Houllier hadn't come back after his heart attack I think Thommo would have taken the club forward. That didn't happen and eventually the manager had to go.

Replacing him with Rafa was a good choice and he did well for a time. Winning the Champions League in your first year is an incredible achievement. He also brought us plenty of other great days and nights such as the 2006 FA Cup final, the wins over Chelsea in three consecutive semi-finals and the 4-1 victory at Old Trafford. They were all brilliant occasions.

Having come from La Liga it was only natural that he would try to bring in players he knew and he had mixed success with that. Despite our first meeting not going too well, I was delighted with the signing of Alonso. I knew the Basque mentality he would bring, he was a fighter and wouldn't shirk the challenge. His first season was very impressive. He did go off the boil for a spell a few years later and I think that may have been because Barcelona had been in contact with his agent. Again though, he showed great character to come good and the team hasn't been the same since he left in 2009.

Josemi was a no from the start, he just wasn't good enough. Albert Riera was also someone I didn't think could be up to scratch because he wasn't able to cut it at Man City. Surely if he couldn't do it for them he wouldn't be good enough for us.

Initially he did well, though, and gave the team width before fading away. He has talent, I think his problem is he doesn't have enough heart.

Luis Garcia provided a lot more than those two but I never thought he was good enough to be a regular starter. He just gave the ball away far too often. Being an impact player would have been his best role. I liked what he could do and he scored some great goals, such as that stunner against Chelsea at Old Trafford. But there were other days when he'd concede possession again and again on the edge of our box. He drove me mad. Having said that, I'll always have a soft spot for him after what he did for us. It's safe to say he'll always receive a warm welcome at Anfield.

THE GHOST PENALTY

We all remember Garcia most for his semi-final winner against Chelsea at Anfield in 2005. It was probably a marginal decision, but I would say the ball was definitely over the line. I think the ref gave it because he didn't want to send Petr Cech off. Everyone seems to forget that in the build-up to that incident we could have had a penalty and Cech should have been dismissed.

'The ghost goal', as Mourinho called it, is often discussed. The fact that Chelsea could have been down to ten men for most of the game seems to have been erased from history. If we had scored the penalty we would have been 1-0 up with a numerical advantage for 86 minutes. I would have preferred that. In a way the ref messed up and let them off. Mourinho should have thanked him for that, not complained.

A TALE OF TWO FERNANDOS

Fernando Morientes was probably the biggest disappointment of all the Spaniards Rafa brought in. At Monaco and Real Madrid he had a lot of style and quality and scored goals, good goals too. I was really excited when he signed but it became obvious very quickly that English football was simply too fast for him. I think it was true, because he scored goals again when he went back to Spain with Valencia.

After that experience I had my doubts about Fernando Torres. If I'm totally honest I thought we should have signed Darren Bent that summer instead. Of all the strikers we were linked with I thought he was the best natural goal-scorer, and he's still doing it in the Premier League now. Thankfully I was wrong about Torres, he's exceeded all my expectations and I'm sure he will continue to find the net regularly in the future. He's a brilliant player.

Someone else who has also firmly erased my fears about their ability is Pepe Reina. During his first season, 2005/06, I thought he was a decent keeper who was liable to make a mistake at times.

Then he had that 'Coco the clown' moment at Goodison Park at the start of his second year when he juggled the ball and allowed Andy Johnson to score. After that I thought he was going to go on to be worse than Jerzy Dudek. I was wrong though. Since then he has shown himself to be incredibly strong mentally, and a great keeper too.

He must have taken a lot of stick after that high profile error, yet he didn't let it affect him. In my opinion only Ray Clemence has been better for Liverpool than Pepe. He's already surpassed Bruce Grobbelaar.

All of those players made some contribution, be it good or bad, during Rafa's reign. For a time, particularly when we finished second in 2008/09 it looked like everything was going in the right direction.

However, I think some mistakes in the transfer market cost us that league title. Torres missed a lot of games that season and if we had a decent back-up striker that would have been the difference. I will discuss Robbie Keane in another chapter. Even before he arrived we had decent strikers who were let go. I would have kept Peter Crouch and Craig Bellamy. When Bellamy signed I thought it would be a mistake, that he was a nuisance. But I'd misjudged Craig.

I spoke to him at a Christmas party and we had a good chat. He was a nice fella who loves sport. I thought if Rafa had nurtured him he could have been a great player for us. Letting him go seemed to be the wrong option. Decisions like that were very similar to Gerard Houllier's last few years and reminded me of how he passed up on the chance to keep Nicolas Anelka.

We all knew Rafa didn't have much money to spend each summer, especially when you compared us to Chelsea or United. But I felt he would have been better buying someone for £10m or £12m instead of buying two or three players on the cheap such as the likes of Sebastian Leto or Mark Gonzalez. At least then you were adding one high quality player each time. It got to a stage where we weren't strengthening the squad anymore; we seemed to be weakening it instead. That was proven to everyone when we finished seventh in 2009/2010.

EIGHT GAMES IN WHICH I SCORED FOR SOCIEDAD

1. A brace vs Real Madrid, Spanish Cup, October 1989. (My first goals for the club)

2. A brace vs Barcelona, October 1989. (I netted twice to help us earn a 2-2 draw after we'd been 2-0 down)

3. One vs Real Madrid, November 1989. (A 2-1 win on a waterlogged pitch. Really the game should have been called off)

4. Another brace vs Barca, Spanish Cup, January 1990. (We drew 3-3 but lost 4-3 on aggregate in extra-time at the Nou Camp)

5. A brace vs Rayo Vallecano. (The sixth consecutive league game in which I scored; no one had ever done that for Sociedad)

6. Yet another brace against Barca. (A load of Kopites had travelled to the Nou Camp and watched us draw 2-2)

7. One vs Real Madrid at the Bernabeu. Dalian and I both got on the scoresheet in a brilliant 3-2 triumph.

8. As usual, a brace vs Barca, May 1991. Dalian scored one and I got two as we won 3-1 in the Nou Camp on the day Barca picked up the league championship trophy.

SOCIEDAD YEARS: EIGHT FOREIGN PLAYERS IN SPAIN

1. *Paolo Futre (Atletico Madrid)*
2. *Hugo Sanchez (Real Madrid)*
3. *Toni Polster (Sevilla)*
4. *Ronald Koeman (Barcelona)*
5. *Jose Luis Chilavert (Real Zaragoza)*
6. *Renat Desayev (Sevilla)*
7. *Kevin Moran (Sporting Gijon)*
8. *Kevin Richardson, Dalian Atkinson (Real Sociedad)*

EIGHT SPANISH LIVERPOOL PLAYERS

1. *Fernando Torres*
2. *Xabi Alonso*
3. *Luis Garcia*
4. *Pepe Reina*
5. *Alvaro Arbeloa*
6. *Albert Riera*
7. *Antonio Nunez*
8. *Josemi*

EIGHT GREAT MOMENTS FROM THE RAFA YEARS

1. *Istanbul (nothing else compares)*
2. *The first Chelsea semi*
3. *The second Chelsea semi*
4. *Cardiff '06*
5. *Athens (great to get there even if a big disappointment)*
6. *The 4-1 against United, 2009*
7. *Beating the European champions at the Nou Camp, 2007*
8. *Olympiakos 2004 (great night)*

CHAPTER 8: THINGS GOING WRONG

LOSING IT

Name: John Aldridge

Occupation: Football commentator for Radio City 96.7 and Liverpool legend.

Secondary School: New Heys Comprehensive

Years at school: Until 1974.

Favourite teacher: Mr Leeson. He was our year head and an alright guy.

Describe your school in three words: "Not much fun."

Best moment: Getting in the school team.

Worst moment: Getting expelled.

Education Q & A, Liverpool Echo.co.uk

USA '94: A page from one of my scrapbooks

A CHIP OFF THE OLD BLOCK

November 1983, Hull vs Newport:

I had to quickly get my dad out of Boothferry Park. I'd been annoyed by my sending off in the first half against Hull, he was even more angry about it and decided to tell the officials what he thought they'd done wrong. That didn't really involve words, just punching the referee in the changing room after the game.

My dad always told me never to let anybody walk over me. He also said if I was ever in a fight to get the first blow in because the other lad wouldn't hesitate to do the same.

He'd done some boxing in his youth and plenty of street fighting. He liked a row. Head-butting them in the nose and walking away was one of his favourite tactics when he needed to defend himself. If the worst came to the worst, I used my elbow to get me out of a scrape on the pitch.

FEELING THE HEAT

When I lose my temper my character can change completely. Millions of people around the world will testify to that after they witnessed me having a disagreement with an official at USA '94.

I got fined $2,500 for the bust-up on the sidelines during our game with Mexico. Jack (Charlton) had got involved too, and he was hit with a $12,500 fine.

Jack's a bit tight at times so he wasn't happy about that but he never had to pay it. When the news came through about the fine a whip-round was done in Ireland, in pubs and clubs all over the country. Around 100,000 Irish punt was collected.

That money actually ended up going to charity because the FAI took care of the fines.

Probably every football fan has seen the footage of me on the sideline that day; it's nearly even more famous than that damn penalty miss against Wimbledon.

Even before the game started that day we'd found ourselves in a ridiculous situation: a midday kick-off in the humidity of Florida against the Mexicans, who were from just around the corner. That was plain stupidity on FIFA's part. We couldn't sunbathe in conditions like that, never mind play football.

Naturally the Mexicans thrived in it and were 2-0 up in the second half. Jack decided to make a double substitution to try and get us back in the game. Tommy Coyne came off and Jason McAteer went on. Then Stan (Steve Staunton) went off too. He was frazzled by the heat; pure red and looking like a turkey.

I went to jog on the pitch in his place but this official wouldn't let me. To this day I don't know why. We were already losing by two goals, now we were down to ten men for no reason.

I completely lost the plot. To make matters even worse the ball never went out of play for about four minutes. While the game was carrying on I went at the official.

"Fuck this and c**t this and dickhead that," I screamed. Everything came out, words I didn't even know I had in my vocabulary. I didn't imagine the cameras would be on me.

When I saw the footage afterwards even I was shocked. I had to admit I looked like a raving lunatic. One newspaper, which I won't mention, had 'Helldridge' as their big headline. They were right because I was like the devil at that stage.

But it meant that by the time I did come on I was so fired up I managed to get on the end of Jason's cross to score a header. We thought it was only a consolation as we lost 2-1, but it turned out to be the one that got us through to the knock out stages on goal difference.

The rest of the squad all had a good laugh about the incident later on that night.

They all loved it. They know me well, and know that's what I'm like when I lose it.

Unfortunately FIFA weren't so understanding.

LOSING IT AT LIVERPOOL

"You shit on me Kenny," I fumed.

It was August 1989 and I was arguing with the boss. I'd injured my arm by elbowing an opponent in a friendly in Sweden. Clearly Kenny wasn't impressed.

A few days later we were preparing for the Charity Shield game with Arsenal. The team for that match was playing against those not going to be in the side. I was in the second XI, a sure sign I would be on the bench. Afterwards Roy Evans told me I was playing for the reserves at Stafford Rangers that same night. I did, but found it highly insulting. I thought I deserved better than that, I deserved a bit more respect. I shouldn't have had to play twice in the same day, especially at 29 years of age. I told Kenny this, and a lot more, the next morning and we had a massive row about it. I knew it wasn't a good situation and, thinking about it now, I should have realised my time at the club was nearing its end.

Apart from the boss I never had too many bust-ups with colleagues during my time at Anfield. Anything that did go on was only minor and usually caused by the competitive nature within the group. Everyone wanted to play. That was impossible, so some tension from time to time was understandable.

There was one particular Friday when we were training and I, as usual, was wound up. Ronnie Moran would never let us tackle each other the day before a game, in case we picked up an injury, but Alan Hansen had been giving me some stick. Everyone was afraid of Jockey. Not because he was a hard man but because he was the captain and had been there for a long time. Paul Walsh used to go mad because Jockey would be kicking him in training. "You're fucking always kicking me," Walshy used to say in his Cockney accent.

Then there was a 50-50 ball between me and Alan. I got there first and won it, but I let Jockey have it too. I mullered him. Ronnie went berserk at me as Jockey fell to the floor. I think I caught him unawares. Walshy loved me for it. I was his new best mate and he rewarded me with loads of free ale.

Plenty of winding up went on at the club, with Jockey usually involved. Sometimes it went too far though, such as the day Craig Johnston tried to take the piss out of me in the pub after training. I didn't like it and used some of my Garston dialect to put him straight. After that there was never a problem again. I think those two moments earned me a lot of respect from the other lads. They knew I wasn't to be messed with.

Neither of those incidents ever went any further than shouting and finger-pointing. But when Phil Thompson and Wayne Harrison fell out, a punch up was definitely going to happen. Wayne was a player who had been brought in from Oldham as a 17-year-old. Manchester United were supposed to have had him signed up before Liverpool pinched him at the last minute. He was a nice lad but wasn't the player that everyone expected him to be.

Maybe that was part of the problem with Thommo, he always wants the best for Liverpool and was probably frustrated by the fact that Wayne wasn't up to it. One day I was injured in a training game and had been walking around the pitch when I had to break them up. They were getting ready to thump each other. I don't know what caused it.

You see Jamie Carragher doing that now and again, having a go at team-mates. Without it going too far, I wish it happened more. It shows people care.

BLOOD AND GUTS
My temper was always on the verge of boiling over when I played in Spain because of the rough treatment defenders dished out. On the opening day of my second season with Sociedad we faced Real Zaragoza and it was particularly bad. We won and I managed to score the only goal of the game. But I received some terrible treatment.

One defender in particular, Alfonso Fraile, had been man marking me and was just taking me out without even attempting to win possession. He even punched me. I ended up covered in blood on my shirt, shorts... everywhere . I was getting pretty wound up and when the ball went out of play I took my opportunity for revenge by elbowing him in the face. I hit him so hard that my arm was bleeding, but I managed to cover it so the ref couldn't figure out what had caused the incident.

After the final whistle all of their players came looking for me and making threats. One was running a finger across his throat to indicate what fate awaited me and muttering *muerte en su casa*, which basically meant they were going to come looking for me. I didn't want to wait. I wanted to sort it on the spot and invited them to do so in the tunnel. They wouldn't accept the offer.

When it came to travelling to their place a few months later they hadn't forgotten about it. One of my team-mates, Lumbreras, had spent some time with Zaragoza and was still in touch with his former colleagues. The message from their camp was that they would definitely have revenge.

I told him to call them and say: "Whoever tries to take me out first must do a proper job. Because if he doesn't, he'll regret it and get the same as what Fraile got." Inside I was afraid but I thought that my best tactic was to play them at their own game. To be honest, I was worried sick before the match. But I must have expressed my anger very well because after all they'd said, I didn't have any problems at all on the day. In fact, they were friendly to me and played in a much fairer manner than before.

GAME OF FRUSTRATION

During my career I always tried my best not to fall out with my team-mates. Sometimes, though, it was impossible. At Sociedad I always played up front on my own. It led to days where I'd barely see the ball. The worst game was against

Valencia away, when we lost 3-1. I think I touched the ball a dozen times in 90 minutes and half of those were flick-ons to no-one in particular.

Afterwards me and a few of the lads went for a few drinks. I was still in a bad mood because of what had happened, or not happened, on the pitch and a team-mate called Dave Villabona was really getting on my nerves. I told him I'd give him a smack if he didn't shut up. "Go on then," he replied so I hit him in the face. I regretted it straight away because he was a cracking lad and a good friend. It just showed how angry I'd been after the match.

I also got in a fight after a Tranmere game at Derby County. Some people were giving me stick in the players' lounge and I asked them to step outside. When we did, it ended up in a free for all with five of them.

NO DEFENCE

I didn't argue with any of the red cards I received during my career. They all came about because I'd lost my cool and they were all justified.

It meant that when I became a manager I was more sympathetic with those who did get sent off... sometimes.

Those who were naïve when it came to doing something wrong annoyed me. In my playing days I usually tried to make sure the referee couldn't see what I was doing, although obviously I didn't always get away with it.

At Tranmere lots of the lads got sent off. It happened so often the fans' favourite chant became: "We only need ten men". I had installed an in-your-face style, where we closed down the opposition all over the park. So we would get lots of bookings for being over-zealous. I had no problem with that. My only problem was when people were getting red cards for stupid things.

It got so bad that I told the players if someone had wound them up to get revenge in the tunnel after the match, rather than during the game. That way you couldn't really get punished for it. After I had told them that, the next match was against Norwich City at home. It was a close contest and a bit feisty on the pitch.

In the tunnel afterwards a 22-man brawl took place. Gary Jones lamped one of their players and it all went off. As the manager I ended up getting involved too. It was mayhem. If you give footballers a little bit of leeway they will definitely take it! Loads of incidents went on in the tunnel. There was always banter and fighting. Emotions run high at the end of games and it can get aggressive in there. I've been on both sides, as the one taking it and dishing it out.

SHOWING DISRESPECT

I once ended up having a major bust-up with Gary Megson down the tunnel at Prenton Park.

When I first became player-manager at Tranmere I used to talk with Gary on the phone quite a lot, because we were all in a difficult situation as bosses in lower leagues. I'd even sold some players to him at Stockport, lads like Eric Nixon and Paul Cook.

When we went to play them at their place our striker David Kelly was injured, but he had travelled with us and got chatting to some of his former team-mates before kick-off. He came back in to the dressing room and said: "Gaffer, be careful today, Megson has told his centre-halves to rough you up. He's told them to try and get you sent off, by standing on you when you're on the floor or making you lose your temper." I wasn't impressed.

I scored to put us 1-0 up and we got to half-time still ahead. But by the end we'd lost 3-1. We had played well; they'd been slightly better. I was still pissed off about what Gary had told his players to do so when he came over to shake my hand I said: "Get in that tunnel. Those two big centre-backs couldn't take me out and you won't either."

"What are you on about?" he asked.

"You shithouse", I replied.

Whenever we came across each other again there was no love lost. He'd completely disrespected me and you don't do that. I was especially disappointed because he knew himself how hard a job it was being manager of a football club. I had enough problems to deal with. The last thing I needed was for a fellow manager to be making life more difficult for me like this.

The feud continued when Megson was manager of West Brom and they were near the top of the league. We got a last minute equaliser at Prenton Park to earn a 2-2 draw. I was delighted, and spotted him running up the tunnel at the end. I thought: "This is my chance" as I sprinted up after him.

I felt so strongly about what had went on that I tried to push him into one of the side rooms to confront him. But he managed to get his hands around the door frame and clung on to prevent me dragging him inside.

I eventually stopped tugging at him and said: "Come into the office and talk about getting your players to do me in." But he wouldn't, he refused.

STANDING UP FOR CLINT

It's not just opposition managers that have caused me to lose my temper, players on other teams have done so too, even those not actually out on the playing field.

During our Worthington Cup final with Leicester City in 2000 Clint Hill was sent off. I was stood on the touchline near the Royal Box trying to re-organise our ten men. As Clint was leaving the pitch I saw Theo Zagorakis, one of Leicester City's subs who was right by me, clapping the red card and nodding his head in agreement.

This was the probably the biggest day of Clint's life and Zagorakis was applauding the fact that it had ended early. So I instantly jumped up and shouted, "Fuck off" as I slapped him on the side of the head.

I'd forgotten that all of the FA big shots were sitting in the Royal Box looking directly down on me. I was later called in front of them. I said I couldn't understand why a fellow professional would be happy about the fact that a young lad playing at Wembley for the first time had been dismissed. I thought it was very wrong and not in the spirit of the game at all.

I apologised to Zagorakis afterwards, to a certain degree. But he shouldn't have done it. I apologised to the FA too. To be fair they didn't hit me with a big fine; it was roughly £1,000.

I think they realised where I was coming from so didn't hit me with a huge cost.

PLAYING WITH AN EXTRA MAN

Even though they knew my limits my own players were good at winding me up too. Everyone remembers our game with Sunderland in the fourth round of the FA Cup in 2000. We accidentally brought on a substitute to replace Clint Hill who had just been sent off, again.

Afterwards a lot of people accused us of cheating and said that something like that could only have happened deliberately. That was a load of rubbish, it happened because I lost it completely on the sideline.

We were winning 1-0 with about two minutes to go when Clint brought down Alex Rae and Rob Harris just gave a free-kick. But the linesman kept flagging so the ref went over, had a word and showed Clint his second yellow card of the game. My assistant, Kevin Sheedy, asked what we were going to do. Quickly, I decided to get Reuben Hazell on and Andy Parkinson off. So Sheeds got the form out and tried to sort the substitution. Reuben started to undo his tracksuit top only to find he had no shirt on underneath. He'd left it in the dressing room. I started slaughtering him about being so negligent and unprofessional and Sheeds was pulling me back.

"What do we now?" he asked again.

"Fraily, get on quick", I roared and gestured at him to get ready.

Stephen Frail was stripped off in a second and ran on.

I was still moaning at Reuben while Clint walked down the tunnel to the dressing room. When the game resumed Sunderland knocked the free-kick into the box and it looked like Jody Craddock was about to head the ball in, before Fraily bravely managed to get it away.

I looked and thought: "Brilliant, well done Fraily". Then in the corner of my eye I spotted Andy Parkinson still on there.

"Fucking hell," I thought as everything started to go off around us. Sunderland had also just realised what was happening. "By the way, we're fucked here," I said to Sheeds as I sat down on the bench. The final whistle blew a few seconds later.

The whole problem had come about because the fourth official had lost concentration when he was trying to drag me away from Reuben.

I'd lost it completely and so had Sheeds. That's why the substitution was never done properly, that's where the problem occurred and why the ref lost track of what was going on. Rob Harris never refereed again. It was very sad for him.

Peter Reid, their manager – he's a good mate of mine – came in to see Sheeds and me afterwards and had a beer with us. "Don't worry Aldo," he said as we chatted about it, "your lads deserved it anyway. It's no problem."

Then he shook our hands and went out again. We thought that was pretty good of him. But after that he went straight into Rob Harris' room and tried to get the game replayed.

People accused us of planning it all. That's ridiculous, how would you do something like that deliberately? It's nonsense. It was just a massive mistake.

From my point of view I just couldn't believe Reuben had been so stupid. I was worried that the FA might do something about it.

But because it was a massive oversight from the officials the authorities saw sense and didn't try to punish us.

HENRY...

I might no longer be a player or manager, that doesn't stop me wanting to kick the TV in when I see the ridiculous decisions officials make on a regular basis.

The worst in recent times was Thierry Henry getting away with that double handball to set up a goal against Ireland for William Gallas in the second leg of the World Cup play-off in November, 2009. Maybe if the striker had used his hand just once you could get over the ref missing it. For him to do it twice and get away with it is unforgivable. Never mind putting my foot through the screen, I wanted to chuck the TV out of the window. Ultimately France endured a horrific World Cup, maybe that was karma.

It still doesn't make up for the fact they, and in particular Henry, were allowed to take part in it in the first place. The striker should have been banned for the whole tournament. It wouldn't have made up for Ireland missing out on the competition, but it would have given people some sense of justice.

By not doing that Sepp Blatter and Michel Platini were endorsing cheating. They were saying you can con people to get to the World Cup and it's okay. Kids who saw that would have gone out and practiced using their hand to make or score goals.

A lot of people in Ireland and beyond wanted France to do poorly during the summer in South Africa. I didn't. I wanted them to win the World Cup, because that would have really embarrassed FIFA and UEFA.

If it had been Wayne Rooney involved, or a star from another country, I'm certain they would have been punished for the incident. Perhaps because Henry is French he wasn't. The fact that it came just after the decision to seed teams in the play-offs was suddenly announced poured more salt into the wound.

Nothing should shock us when UEFA are involved though, because they can be absolutely useless. We all saw how poorly they organised the 2007 Champions League final in Athens between AC Milan and Liverpool.

The ticketing and turnstile operation was so bad that night it was a miracle some serious trouble or fatalities didn't occur. They simply don't care about fans; they're only interested in lining their own pockets.

It wasn't just the Irish football team that UEFA or the French cheated either, it was the whole country. Financially, Ireland is in a mess right now and it would have given the whole place a huge lift if they had made it to South Africa. Businesses would have thrived on the people supporting their team.

CHANGING THE RULES

Martin Hansson, the referee that night at the Stade de France, obviously made a catastrophic error. In such circumstances a timeout to examine exactly what's happened should be allowed. It's not going to make a big difference. The ball had gone dead so why not have a word with the fourth official and assess it all rationally. I accept that referees can't see everything. Therefore being able to discuss different situations would obviously help them reach the correct conclusion.

If that facility had been in use at the 1988 FA Cup final I wouldn't have missed that penalty because Brian Hill never would have awarded it. The tackle on me was fair. An earlier foul was definitely a spot-kick. Maybe he was trying to make up for not awarding that decision or for the fact that Peter Beardsley's 'goal' was disallowed. Either way it doesn't matter, I still took the penalty and missed.

Being able to handle pressure is important for refs as much as footballers now. I think that pressure is increasing every year and every little decision they make is being scrutinised. One way to help them would be to make them declare to the FA which team they supported when they were younger.

As kids they would have been a fan of a team and, no matter what people say, you can't really take that away from someone. I think their allegiance comes into play when they are making 50/50 decisions.

The team they supported might not even be playing in that particular game, but the outcome might still affect their chances of success. I think that enters their heads. I know if I was a referee and there was a call to be made that somehow helped Liverpool I'd give it in their favour, damn right I would. You see those type of calls every weekend.

I know certain referees that don't like Liverpool, it's obvious. Each time they take charge of a game they make calls against us. I know I'm right on this. Part of that is because they followed Manchester United or Everton when they were younger. If you knew where their allegiances lay, or used to lie, you could prevent them from having anything to do with a game involving that club, or other fixtures that affected that same club. The same applies to referees who may have supported Liverpool. It works both ways.

Having former players as refs is often suggested and I think it would work. Because you've played you know what players do and how to judge situations that aren't entirely clear-cut. Steve Baines, who played for Chesterfield and a few other clubs, took charge of some of our games at Tranmere and I found him to be very good. The only downside to that solution is ex-players are even more open to accusations of helping their old clubs.

BEING FRANK, IT'S A JOKE

No matter what the background of the man with the whistle it's clear that they should be able to benefit from the use of technology. I don't see any reason for not using replays or goal-line computers to tell us if the ball has gone in or not. I can't understand why FIFA are against it. They've embraced the idea of extra officials behind the goals – sometimes with dodgy tracksuits on. So why not go a step further.

The World Cup proved that something desperately needs to be done. Frank Lampard's disallowed 'goal' in the game against Germany was a joke. The ball was clearly well over the line and nobody saw it. That highlighted that at the very least we need extra officials on the pitch to help make those key decisions. Mistakes like that can cost games. Who knows how that match would have turned had that goal been allowed? What is certain is that it is embarrassing to see those type of blunders taking place. How can such a blatant oversight occur in the biggest sporting tournament in the world? It's crazy. I see FIFA have now at least ratified the use of extra goal-line officials in the UEFA Champions League for the next two seasons after the experiment in the Europa League. Like I say, I would like to see them go the whole way and embrace technology too.

Action replays could also be used to cut out diving. It makes me sad whenever I see footballers throw themselves to the floor without being touched. No one could ever call me a diver, although plenty of defenders tried to. Instead of diving I'd wait until a 50/50 ball came into the box. If my opponent was naïve enough to go for it I'd try to get there first. If I did I knew I'd get a penalty because he'd take me out. That was definitely a foul and not a dive.

Whenever I'm watching football now and my missus is in the room hoovering you'll see players like Cristiano Ronaldo or Didier Drogba fall over if she accidentally knocks against the TV. That's the way the game has gone. It is cheating and the authorities have to stamp down on it in a big way now. It spoils football for everyone. A three or four game ban for anyone caught diving would solve it.

I would probably go a step further by fining the managers of players who dive or act the way Henry did a week's wages. If a manager were coughing up because of his players those antics would soon stop. Can you imagine Alex Ferguson or someone like that standing for those types of incidents then? I don't think they would allow it to happen ever again.

PUTTING MY FOOT IN IT

I'll finish off this chapter with an amusing tale that shows how sometimes you just have to laugh when you end up losing the plot in football. It was when I was a player at Tranmere. We were playing Oldham at their place.

I got sent off and quite rightly, too. I could have no arguments with the referee's decision. I left the pitch and was so wound up that when I got back to the visitors' changing room, I took my frustration out on the door by booting it with all my strength.

One of my team-mates Ged Brannan was in the changing room at the time. He had just come off injured and was up on the treatment table being attended to by Les Parry, who was the physio then. Ged was just lying there, he said, and the next thing he saw was this boot come through the door.

I had kicked it so hard that my foot went straight through the other side. Ged said it was like a scene from a cartoon to see this leg appear from nowhere. I thought it was a big wooden door and hadn't thought twice about kicking it.

That made us all laugh but the story didn't end there. I think Sharpy – Graeme Sharp – was the Oldham boss at the time and they ended up sending me a bill for the door. I had to pay it, of course, I could have no complaints about that.

EIGHT THINGS THAT HAVE DRIVEN ME MAD

1. Thierry Henry's blatant cheating in Paris
2. Fernando Torres being substituted early at Birmingham by Rafa in 2009. Stevie's expression said it all
3. Luis Garcia constantly giving the ball away
4. Club owners who take football fans for a ride
5. Callers trying to wind me up on the phone-in!
6. Harry Kewell. Someone who had all the ability but didn't seem to want it enough at Liverpool
7. Players who wave their hands or make gestures to try and get another player booked
8. That official at USA '94...

MY CAREER DISCIPLINARY RECORD

One red card in Spain
None for Liverpool
Newport – one red
Oxford – sent off maybe 3 times
Tranmere – sent off maybe 3 times too
No red cards for Ireland
Five yellows for Ireland (and 3 of these in 1987)
Being banned from coming on as a sub – one!

8 RED CARDS

1. Hull vs Newport, 1983. 0-0. My dad didn't agree and left the referee in no doubt about how he felt!
2. Real Sociedad vs Sabadell. I scored to end a four game run without a goal before I got my marching orders.
3. Oldham vs Tranmere, 1995. I was so angry I kicked a hole in the door when I got back to the dressing room.
4. Carlisle vs Tranmere, 1997.
5. Steven Gerrard's red card vs Everton, 2005/06.
The lads went on to win 3-1, it was one of our best performances under Rafa.
6. Pepe Reina getting sent off vs Chelsea when it was clear he hadn't touched Arjen Robben in February, 2006
7. Xabi Alonso's dismissal at Highbury in 2006 when he slipped and the ref clearly didn't see what happened.
8. Sami Hyypia getting sent off in the third minute at Old Trafford and us going on to lose 4-0 in April, 2003

CHAPTER 9: WE WILL
NEVER FORGET

96

April 15, 1989...

ALRIGHT ALDO

TRAGEDY

At the end of every day my mind always turns to the events of April 15, 1989. A gloriously sunny afternoon for an FA Cup semi-final against Nottingham Forest at Hillsborough in Sheffield, it should have been a special game.

Instead, it will forever be remembered for the deaths of 96 Liverpool fans. The awful events in the Leppings Lane End of the ground are never far from my thoughts, but before I fall asleep I always take a few minutes to remember those who tragically passed away.

I went to a lot of Liverpool games, home and away, when I was growing up. I remember being at the Baseball Ground in the mid-seventies and we were locked outside before kick-off. The police lost the plot and forced us all into one small space. I was terrified because I thought we were all going to get crushed. "I could die here" was the only thought in my head. I really was afraid. At Anfield, I'd been in the Kop loads of times when the crowd was carrying you from one part to the other. That never felt scary. At Derby I was petrified. The cops eventually opened the gates to let us in and because of that nobody was hurt. In the Leppings Lane End at Hillsborough, the fans weren't so lucky.

Out on the pitch on that tragic day the players didn't have a clue about what was going on. I think a few of us thought a barrier had collapsed in the stand.

Then the ref said we were going into the dressing room because there was nothing we could do about it. If we had known what was really going on we would have stayed out there to try to help. That still angers me, the fact that we couldn't help. Maybe the health and safety people would have wanted us out of the way because we might have been a hindrance. But we could have helped get supporters out of there. We might only have been able to help save one life, but that's still one life.

Like most people I find the day difficult to talk about. It conjures up a lot of emotions, with great sadness obviously being the most obvious. For any supporter to lose their life because they attended a football match is not right. Then to have their memory disrespected adds to the immense suffering.

I won't even mention the name of the newspaper that did the most damage in that respect. Everyone knows what I'm talking about. The editor, again, I won't even use his name, is someone who I still can't stand.

If ever I see him on TV or hear him on the radio I immediately switch over and I would urge anyone who reads this book to do the same. How can anyone try to sell newspapers off the back of a tragedy such as Hillsborough? To do that you must have something seriously wrong with you.

My dad was in the Main Stand at the match that day and he watched fellow Liverpool fans try to help the injured and dying. Having been to hundreds of games myself since 1967 I knew immediately that none of the allegations, which I won't repeat here, were true. It was all lies. That's why fans such as myself, and thousands of others, will never look at a copy of that rag.

Thankfully not everyone reacted so badly to what happened. Others reached out to the city of Liverpool and our football club in a great time of need. I think every club around the country, and some from further afield, sent flowers and their sympathies because they knew it could have been their fans in a similar situation.

Celtic in particular were brilliant. Kenny obviously brought them on board and they really supported us. We went up there to play them in a memorial game at the end of that April and I've never heard YNWA sung with so much passion. It was unbelievable. There were always good relations between the clubs before then but their compassion strengthened the bond.

That was why I couldn't believe it when El-Hadji Diouf spat

at the fans at Parkhead during a UEFA Cup quarter-final in 2003. The club should have kicked him out after that. Rangers were good too; they knew what we were going through because they had experienced a similar disaster at Ibrox in 1971.

REVISITING THE SCENE

I didn't return to Hillsborough until I was Tranmere manager and it wasn't an experience I relished. Everything from that awful day came back to me. I went out on the pitch, had a look at the stand where the Liverpool fans had been and said a little prayer. There was hardly anyone else in the stadium, which suited me. I wanted it to be a private moment.

In the weeks immediately after the disaster not many of us players wanted the season to continue. I even seriously considered retiring. A lot of people said the cup should have been abandoned as a mark of respect. Others wanted us to go all the way and win it for those who had passed away. Playing on wasn't easy but it was probably the right decision. Winning the semi-final against Nottingham Forest was the priority for me because it was at the original tie that the supporters had died at. We did it thanks to a 3-1 victory in which I scored twice. Those were the most important goals I ever netted and it was my own personal way for me to honour the 96.

HONOURED

In April 2010 I was asked to do a reading at the Hillsborough Memorial Service at Anfield. It was a huge honour and very emotional. I was very nervous beforehand. My only worry was about making a mistake; I didn't want to let anybody down. Hopefully I didn't. No matter what people say the events of that day in 1989 will never be forgotten by any of us, and rightly so. The fight for justice goes on and hopefully in the near future those who were at fault will be punished for something that could so easily have been avoided.

BOYS IN GREEN

What, then, when an English friend looks and says: 'Aldo, what's a Scouser doin' playin' for England?'

"I just say it was my granny and if she hadn't been here, I wouldn't be here.

"Playing for Ireland is like being part of a family, that's how we look at it. We're a family, that's why we do so well, because we fight for each other.

"We don't want to let each other down and we want to win for Ireland..."

Interview, Irish national newspaper, 1992

Player passes from USA '94
and a cartoon of me in Ireland
kit from one of my scrapbooks...

SHIRT SWAPS

Gianluca Vialli, Fernando Hierro and Alan Hansen are just some of the great names I've swapped shirts with. Now all those souvenirs sit in a room of my house. I've also got one from former Germany player Stefan Kuntz; trust me to end up with that! I didn't even realise it was his until after the game and I looked at it in the dressing room.

I never planned or hoped to exchange shirts with anyone, unlike some of the lads who would be ripping the kit off the most famous opponents we came up against. Even when I obtained Vialli's he came to me about it first, a fact that amazed both my Irish team-mates and myself.

The sides were standing in the tunnel getting ready to go out, with me at the back of the line. Vialli walked the whole way down, past all the lads, until he got to me.

Then he said: "John my socks, shorts and shirt for your socks, shorts and shirt after the game."

Naturally I was delighted and agreed straight away. At the time Vialli was one of the best players in the world and that is one of the most precious items I have from my career. I've also got signed shirts from Maradona and Pele, which I bought. I wanted to swap shirts with some of the Brazil team, but they arrogantly all refused after Ireland beat them 1-0 in Dublin. I think they were too upset by the result. The vast majority of those shirts in my collection came from playing for my country, which is one of my proudest achievements.

THANKFULLY ENGLAND DIDN'T PICK ME

International football wasn't something I had much reason to worry about until March 1986. Instead, I'd just been concentrating on scoring goals for my clubs. When I started to do that on a regular basis to help Oxford United reach the First Division there were one or two suggestions that England should pick me.

They mainly came from people at the club. I don't think anyone else was talking up my chances. In my own mind I felt there was no way I'd be called up by England when they had players such as Gary Lineker already in the line-up. Just because I'd done well for an unfashionable team wasn't going to alter that fact. I understood such reasoning.

Plus, I also thought I was already in my mid to late twenties and no international manager would pick me at that stage of my career. Looking back now I think it's the way it was meant to be. Thankfully England never came in for me and Ireland did.

At Oxford, I was very friendly with Dave Langan who was from Dublin, played for Ireland and always spoke about Irish football. It was his influence that really sparked my interest in the Ireland team; from then on I always looked out for their results and wanted them to win. I qualified for the country through my mother's side of the family. Her gran originally came from Athlone, on the banks of the River Shannon right in the middle of the country, before they moved to Merseyside. This link was something I was aware of, even if I hadn't looked into it too much. When I did it became clear that I could wear a green jersey. Initially it looked like I might get a cap under Eoin Hand until he was sacked. With Jack Charlton taking charge I wasn't sure if I would get picked, but that concern turned out to be unnecessary.

He came to watch Oxford face Aston Villa in the semi-final of the Milk Cup and hung around for a chat in the players' lounge afterwards, where he asked me if I wanted to be part of his squad. I already knew the answer to that question and also told him about Ray Houghton's Irish links. Jack hadn't been aware of that connection and quickly went about securing Ray's services too.

It took us both a while to become comfortable with the Irish set-up. The first time I travelled to Dublin for a game with Wales everything was new to me and I even got lost in the airport. When I eventually found our hotel I was warmly welcomed by Kevin Moran.

On the pitch, becoming accustomed to Jack's system of play was the first priority and something we did well, even if my future team-mate Rushie scored the game's only goal to inflict a 1-0 defeat on us. What I remember most about the trip was sharing a room with Liam Brady. When I learned I was to be rooming with him, an Irish legend, it made me very nervous. That feeling was completely unnecessary as 'Chippy' was very easy to talk to when he arrived.

That was how I found everyone in the squad. An awful lot of people really focussed on the fact some of us hailed from different places or backgrounds. From what I experienced it never mattered to any one of my team-mates. If anything, it brought us closer together.

The likes of Chippy and Kevin Moran would rally around players like myself. They protected us and always made sure we felt welcome. Myself and Ray, and the other lads who weren't born in Ireland, showed a lot of passion and pride in a green jersey. When people saw that, they appreciated it and knew we cared about the team. The fans were the same.

MISTAKEN IDENTITY

I think my background wasn't a problem for 99 per cent of Irish people. Only on very rare occasions did it become an issue. The first time was in a bar when some fella had a go at me because I was from Liverpool. I ran after him and he disappeared pretty quickly. On another night, in Derry, it led to an argument that we managed to straighten out. But those are the only minor incidents I can recall.

Although there was also a trip to the Galway Races, which I thought was going to end in trouble. The city on the west coast is one of my favourite places in Ireland, especially when the horse racing is on.

A few years ago I was walking towards the racecourse entrance when I noticed a young lad standing nearby, drinking a can of beer and staring intently at me.

As I got closer he kept looking at me and I was preparing myself for some trouble.

He eventually blurted out the words: "Steve Staunton".

I, and everyone else with me, erupted with laughter because he thought I was Stan. It was a hilarious. A few people have understandably mixed me up with Rushie over the years, but only once have I been confused with Stan. In general I've found everywhere in Ireland to be friendly and welcoming.

A prime example is when I am in Dublin and go out for a pint. Before I've finished my drink, the barman will put down another one in front of me. I'll tell him I haven't ordered anything. He'll point down to the other end of the room and say: "It's from that lad down there. He wants to thank you for all you've done for Ireland."

It's my huge pleasure to accept a kind gesture like that. The people are great, very warm and friendly. If I'm out on the streets or in shops people always say hello or have a laugh and a joke. Every trip to Ireland is a joy.

NORTHERN IRELAND

The same couldn't be said of our visit to Windsor Park in November 1993. During my career I played in a lot of stadiums where it was really hostile, Turkey was one of the most intimidating places I ever visited. But Windsor Park that night surpassed all of them. It was eerie. Billy Bingham had stoked the fire between the two countries by saying the Republic's players weren't Irish. I think he was wrong to do that. There was already enough political tension around the game; it didn't need a manager to say anything else.

One incident I remember as we were travelling to the game puts it all into perspective about how the situation was at that time. Getting us to the ground was a huge security operation. As our coach made its way to Windsor Park, we were flanked by armoured cars with helicopters circling overhead. As we passed a synthetic pitch with floodlights on, with the coach meandering along, a few young lads came over firing pretend machine guns at us, which we thought was quite funny.

Then a bit further down – I was talking to Andy Townsend at the time – we saw a woman walking across the road with two kids. What happened next sent a shiver down my spine. As the woman saw us coming, she turned her back and turned the kids' heads in the opposite direction so that they couldn't see the Republic of Ireland coach passing by. That was a pretty eerie moment and highlighted how things were back in those days.

The police were taking no chances when it came to the potential for trouble. We all knew it was going to be a tough place to go to get a result, and that fact was rammed home to us when we went out for the warm-up. None of our fans were allowed inside the stadium. If any did get in they had to stay silent.

Not having them there was a strange feeling. Windsor Park had yet to be redeveloped then, and a strong wind blew right across the pitch. With the North being backed by a passionate home crowd, who were really encouraged on the touchline by Bingham just prior to kick-off, we knew a difficult evening could be in store. To be fair to their players a lot of them wanted us to qualify for the World Cup and they told us so afterwards. However, they obviously couldn't show that in their performance, and definitely didn't in what turned out to be a non-event of a first half. Neither side managed to create much at all until Jimmy Quinn volleyed in a brilliant strike with just over a quarter of an hour remaining. At that stage it looked grim for us.

Thankfully Alan McLoughlin had come on as a sub and he smashed in a great shot from the edge of the box after a Denis Irwin free-kick had only been half cleared. "Alan, Alan, who the fuck is Alan?" the Ireland supporters memorably sang in honour of him later on. The fans partied that night and so did the squad. I couldn't because I had 'flu and went straight to bed instead of going out. I didn't even have one pint to mark us reaching our second successive World Cup. The lads obviously had plenty, if the noise they made when returning at five or six in the morning was anything to go by.

GREAT DAYS AND NIGHTS

I might have missed out on that session but usually I was right in the middle of our numerous nights out. The best celebration came after we beat England in Stuttgart at Euro '88. Normally, Jack would let us drink until midnight if we had another game coming up a few days later. On that occasion he let us stay up until 12.30am.

Defeating Bobby Robson's side was special. It showed everyone around the world that we had arrived. They took a lot of criticism afterwards, which I felt was unfair. England played well that day and were probably a little unlucky not to get a draw. Packie Bonner had to make some great saves to keep us ahead.

That was probably the finest of the many fantastic results we enjoyed. Beating England always means more, even more than defeating Italy in Giants Stadium in 1994. If you asked me to choose which World Cup was better I would have to say Italia '90. We reached the quarter-finals and I played in a lot more of the games. The fact that, four years later, I scored my first goal in the biggest football competition there is doesn't change my mind. In America I didn't feature that much and the only game I did start, against Norway, is probably one of the worst World Cup games of all time. Absolutely nothing happened in the entire 90 minutes.

Being left out for our second round game against Holland hurt me at the time. Looking back I can see that Jack was probably right to go with Tommy Coyne because he was younger and would have been able to handle the heat better. I felt I might have started because I'd always done well against Ronald Koeman. He didn't like marking me but, knowing the way Jack operated, he probably wasn't aware of that.

PRE-MATCH PREPARATION – THE NAKED TRUTH

A lot was made of how we prepared for games and sometimes it was unusual, especially before we played Russia at Euro '88. I always went for a swim and used the sauna whenever I got to our hotel and did so again.

As I was splashing about these two old guys got into the pool and both of them were naked. Naturally I didn't hang around for long and went to the sauna to get away from them. I think I'd only been sitting in there for a minute when the door opened and a couple came in, both also without any clothes on.

It turned out that we were in a naturist camp. Jack went nuts. We were banned from going into that part of the hotel, not that any of us would have wanted to. Apparently some of the paparazzi turned up when they heard about it. If they had been a day earlier they would have had a picture of us all alongside the naturists.

People often criticised us for being unprofessional or not being serious enough in the build-up to games. I would have to agree with that, even if I would argue that it never affected our performances.

The most memorable of our pre-match sessions probably came in October 1990 during the build up to a European Championship qualifier with Turkey. As usual we all arrived in Dublin on the Sunday and ended up out in Leeson Street in the city centre until 6am in the morning. Normally we would have gone back to the hotel then.

Instead Quinny (Niall Quinn) suggested we go to a 24-hour bar down by the docks. We ended up there having a few more pints until about 8.30am. The dockers couldn't believe it and they also didn't believe we'd be able to play an important game a few days later. Training that afternoon was absolutely farcical; none of us wanted the ball. On the Wednesday we beat Turkey 5-0.

Another regular part of our pre-match routine included a Monday night trip to the cinema in Dublin city centre.

It was a good means of getting out and relaxing, although Ronnie Whelan sometimes took the opportunity to relax in a different way. On the odd occasion, he sneaked out of the cinema and went around the corner for a few games of snooker and a couple of pints of Guinness. All of the Irish players enjoyed themselves and I think that was one of the reasons why we did so well. We could have enjoyed even more success too. Not qualifying for the European Championships in 1992 and 1996 was disappointing.

During each campaign we had set ourselves up to reach the tournament with a good beginning only to not do enough in the last few fixtures. Even after we'd messed up in the group stages for 1996 I still felt we would get there in the play-off, especially because the game with Holland was due to take place at Anfield.

In my own mind I thought it was set up for me to score the winning goal on my home ground.

As usual the Irish fans didn't let us down. They created an atmosphere that matched anything I've ever experienced at Liverpool games. Unfortunately it didn't affect our opponents who had Clarence Seedorf running the midfield and deservedly defeated us 2-0.

A LONG WAIT

As much as I loved playing for Ireland the wait for my first international goal haunted me. I could have saved myself so much worry and stress if I'd converted a penalty against Czechoslovakia during a mini-tournament in Iceland in the summer of 1986. We returned with the trophy after wins over the Czechs and the hosts. It was a satisfying trip for the team. Personally I wasn't content because I'd yet to find the net, a miserable run that would continue until October 1988. A lot of people, including Jack, said I did a good job for the team in a role that wasn't natural to me. That was true but I still got in the box on plenty of occasions. The problem was I was snatching at chances and being tentative in front of goal. I just had no real belief when an opportunity came my way.

If others were trying to pressure me I didn't need it because I always put myself under pressure. Len Ashurst, my boss at Newport County, had correctly told me that if I wanted to be a top striker I had to score at least one goal in every two games. Those were the kind of figures I needed to be registering every season he said. Even at international level I wanted to do that. I always felt that, even if the team was winning, if I didn't score I hadn't done my job.

It was all made worse by the fact that I'd go back to my club a few days later and sometimes score two or three goals without any difficulties. If I had been playing for England I would have been dumped after about a dozen games, there is no way they would have stuck with me. The press would have a made a big deal of it too.

The Irish media didn't mention it that often, and if they did ever bring it up Jack told them to mind their own business. He always insisted I was doing well. That sequence was my longest without scoring for a team, and by a huge distance. I think the most consecutive games I had without hitting the net for a club side was six, or maybe seven. I got in the habit of changing my boots if I went three matches without scoring. I'd give Nike a ring and they'd always send me a new pair.

It was one of the few superstitions I had and I think it worked every time. With Ireland it didn't matter what I did, I could have got new feet and new boots, I still couldn't score. I had goals disallowed for offside and a variety of other reasons. David Kelly netting a hat-trick on his debut against Israel when he started in place of me did little to ease the ever-increasing anxiety.

After going through the 1988 European Championships without it happening I thought the moment would never arrive. Finally, in a friendly against Tunisia in Dublin, it did, mainly thanks to my mate Ray Houghton. He did all the hard work to tee me up for a simple finish from close range. Anyone who witnessed my celebration without having seen the goal would have imagined I'd just netted an absolutely brilliant strike. They couldn't have been more wrong. I didn't care and the crowd shared my delight as they roared with approval. We ended up winning 4-0 in an outing many people will have long forgotten. I'll always remember it.

My first goal in a competitive game came the following year, during our last World Cup qualifier on the tiny island of Malta. Typically, having waited so long to finally put a chance away in competitive action, I scored twice to guarantee us a place at the world's biggest sporting event for the very first time. It might only have been Malta on a terrible pitch, but it's a game I cherish.

For the opener I managed to score a header from a well-worked corner routine and then converted a penalty too. To get those goals that assured of us a World Cup spot was a brilliant feeling, one of the best I've experienced. Unsurprisingly there were a large number of Irish fans present to help us celebrate that night. All of us – players and supporters – spent it in a club.

At one stage I wanted to go to the toilet on the other side of the room. I set off in that direction and the next thing I knew, I was lifted up and carried along by the crowd of Irish fans. They passed me the whole way across to the toilets. They were happy and so were the press, who gave me lots of praise. Eventually I went on to score 19 times for my country in 69 outings. That wasn't a bad ratio when you consider the start I had.

Those two goals on the Mediterranean island were sweet, yet my best effort for Ireland came at USA '94. With everything else that went on that day against Mexico my header was barely noticed. I hadn't even given it much significance in my own mind. I was like a man possessed and had really got amongst the Mexicans. I was swearing at them and using my Spanish to call them every name under the sun. I ruffled them up big time. If the game had continued for another ten minutes I think we would have got a draw.

As I walked off the pitch afterwards I was still so wound up I didn't realise exactly what it meant to the team. Tony Cascarino came up to me and said: "Brilliant Aldo, what a goal." I was bemused by his words because we'd lost. Then he told me: "Because of your header we now only need a draw against Norway to progress to the knockout stages." I was made up.

Unbelievably, there was a time when I only needed one more goal to be Ireland's joint all-time leading scorer along with Frank Stapleton. I should have matched his total of 20. I remember one of my last games against Portugal away and I missed a great chance with my head that I normally would have buried. If I had I would have equalled Frank's total.

ROBBIE KEANE

Even if I had I wouldn't have stayed at the top of the country's all time scorers list for too long. That crown has been firmly grabbed by Robbie Keane.

I don't think any Irish player will ever net more than him. Like a lot of Ireland and Liverpool supporters I was delighted when he moved to Merseyside in 2008. Prior to that transfer I had chatted to Phil Thompson about Robbie on a few occasions and we both agreed he would be a great buy for us. People say it was Rick Parry who signed him rather than Rafa Benitez, I don't know if that's true. What is obvious is that he was treated terribly when he came to the club.

We all waited a while for Robbie to get his first goal for the club before it came against PSV Eindhoven. Then he scored two against West Brom a few weeks later and we all thought he would finally come good. Again it didn't happen.

In December he scored a brilliant goal in the 1-1 draw at Arsenal before following it up with a well-taken brace against Bolton. You could tell he was suddenly confident and I thought he would go on to enjoy a good season from that point. Then the manager left him out for the next game and didn't even bring him on. That was a ridiculous decision.

Goalscorers go on runs; you keep them in the team when they've just scored. You don't rest them.

Something wasn't right from the start of the whole saga. Robbie got a raw deal at Liverpool and I felt very sorry for him. He was a Liverpool supporter and got treated badly by the club he loved. I know how he feels. Later that season, after he'd left, we could have done with him when Fernando Torres was injured and during 2009/10 the same applied. He was better than what we had on the bench. Even if he hadn't been in the starting eleven he would have been a useful squad player.

On the occasions I've met Robbie I've never talked to him about the reasons behind it all. I did speak to him after he left and he was fuming. As a fellow Liverpool fan I apologised to him for how the club had failed to look after him. He kept his silence on it and never came out and criticised Rafa Benitez or anyone else, which would have been understandable. I think the fact he didn't shows how much he still cares about the club and the fans, despite what happened.

CONFIDENT FOR THE FUTURE

When fans of rival teams want to have a go at Liverpool they refer to us as 'the history channel'. In a similar way, people in Ireland are living off memories of past success. We've only had one World Cup appearance since the time I played.

Mick McCarthy did very well getting his side to Korea and Japan in 2002. Since then we have failed to reach a major tournament. Not making it to South Africa hurt the most because of how we were robbed by Thierry Henry.

I spoke to the Irish team kitman a few months after that draw in Paris. He was asked to go into the French dressing room to swap some shirts and said none of them were celebrating; the place was like a morgue. I was pleased to hear that because they knew they'd qualified the wrong way. They probably went into the World Cup with a guilt complex and maybe that was one of the reasons why they did so poorly. That, plus the fact they had one of the worst international football managers I've ever seen. I know quite a few French people and they apologised to me when we spoke. I told them not to because it wasn't their fault.

The qualifying campaign ended sourly for us in Paris. The upside is we only lost one game throughout it, the first leg against the cheating French in Dublin. I think it shows Giovanni Trapattoni has done a tremendous job. Okay, we didn't qualify, but it seems that everything is going in the right way and everyone has a lot of belief in the country's football team again. He's a terrific manager. It's a pity the FAI didn't appoint him instead of Brian Kerr all those years ago.

FAVOURITE GAMES IN WHICH I SCORED FOR IRELAND
1. One vs Mexico at USA 94.
My first World Cup goal. I was a bit fired up for it!
2. One vs Tunisia, October 1988.
A tap-in, but a major relief to finally get off the mark.
3. A brace vs Malta, 1989.
I scored my first competitive international goals to help us qualify for Italia '90.
4. A hat-trick vs Turkey, 1990.
This treble in a Euro '92 qualifier doubled my Eire tally.
5. One vs Albania, 1992.
I was tired going into the May World Cup qualifier as I'd just returned from the Tranmere players' end of season holiday but I still scored.
6. A hat-trick vs Latvia.
'Sheeds' also got on the scoresheet in a 4-0 win.
7. One vs Northern Ireland.
This goal came in a 4-0 win in Belfast, an occasion that was far more pleasant than our 1993 trip to Northern Ireland.
8. Two vs Latvia.
We had to win this Euro 96 qualifier. I got both goals in a 2-1 victory, my last for my country. Unfortunately we didn't make it to the tournament.

ALRIGHT ALDO

8 GREAT IRISH PLAYERS I PLAYED WITH
1. Ronnie Whelan
2. Paul McGrath
3. Ray Houghton
4. Liam Brady
5. Niall Quinn
6. Roy Keane
7. Kevin Sheedy
8. Steve Staunton

CHAPTER 11: MANAGEMENT

BOSS, LA

1. *Bill Shankly*
2. *Jack Charlton*
3. *Bob Paisley*
4. *Kenny Dalglish*
5. *Joe Fagan*
6. *Sir Alex Ferguson*
7. *Jock Stein*
8. *Sir Matt Busby*

*A list of my top eight
football managers...*

Two high profile games from my time as Tranmere boss
– an FA Cup tie against Liverpool and the front page of
the ECHO from the 2000 Worthington Cup final...

TELL ME WHY, KENNY...

I'll never understand Kenny Dalglish's decision to sell me in 1989. As a manager you have to make choices like that. But even now, all these years later, it's something I think about a lot, it's always there in the back of my mind. When I signed for Liverpool it was like getting the best Christmas present I could ever have asked for. Taking that away felt like a kick in the stomach and I'll never get over it.

I've still got the utmost respect for what Kenny did as a manager and a player. But I've never been able to get my head around him transferring me to Real Sociedad. We've met plenty of times in the years since I left and have always got on. There is never a problem between us and I could never say I dislike him. At the same time I'd love for him to sit down some day and tell me his real reasons behind getting rid of me.

A lot of people have told me since, and I agree, that he was wrong. After I left I went on to score another 220 odd goals, proof that I could still do a job. I played until I was 39, so there was never a doubt about my fitness. The fact that he was one of my heroes when I was younger made it all even worse.

When it was obvious Rushie was going to leave, Liverpool needed someone to replace one of British football's top strikers. I came in, waited for my chance and then took it by scoring a lot of goals. To be forced out of the club I loved after doing well was hard to take.

I did tell Kenny I'd stay and fight for my place. He told me I wouldn't be playing because he was going to stick with Rushie and Peter up front, and it would be better if I moved on. The year after I'd left he brought in Ronny Rosenthal. He's a great lad and scored a few. But I don't think he did a better job than I could have.

Despite all that I would still say Kenny was a good manager. He drilled the Liverpool Way into the team and they produced the goods for him on the field. Because of that he didn't need to be a motivator, unlike a lot of the other bosses I worked under. The only time I remember him using motivational tactics was for our FA Cup semi-final against Nottingham Forest in '89, the replay of the Hillsborough game.

Before kick-off in the dressing room he named the side. Then he said that Brian Clough had hoped we'd just lie down and not play the game because of the tragedy. Clough had never won the cup so he wanted a walkover to get into the final. Kenny said there was no way we'd be giving him that.

As we came out of the tunnel we went past Clough and he had clearly had a drink or two. He said to Peter Beardsley: "Young man, you should play for England." By then Peter had about 30 caps. I was already really up for that game, and after Kenny said those words about Clough we were never going to lose.

TACTICAL GENIUS JACK AND CALLING IT A DAY

A lot is made of tactics in the modern game. The best tactician I worked with wasn't Kenny, it was Jack Charlton. He was a genius. At Liverpool the club had the best players. Jack didn't have that. Ireland was his first international job so he'd gone to the Mexico World Cup and watched it closely to learn how international sides played.

He figured we'd never, ever match them in terms of just playing football. So he decided we had to stop them first and foremost. We'd put the ball in the corner and then make them play in their own half. Everyone hated facing us. People say it wasn't great to watch but it was successful. I was happy once we were winning. I probably learnt most from Jack than anyone else. When I took over at Tranmere I wanted to play the same way; with energy and by closing people down all over the park, although I still wanted us to play good football and keep the ball on the floor too.

Some of the bosses I had weren't great when it came to tactics, but I'm sure they were better than I ever was. At times it's not about that either, simple things can make a difference. That was proven to me in what turned out to be my last game for Ireland. Mick McCarthy had succeed Jack by then and we were playing Iceland at home in a qualifier for France '98.

As I'd expected, I was on the bench and watched as the visitors defended in numbers and we struggled to score. With time running out the game was still scoreless and some of the fans started chanting my name.

I was certain Mick would send me on; instead he used Middlesbrough's Alan Moore. As I watched the inevitable 0-0 draw conclude I made my mind up to retire from international football. I informed Mick in the dressing room and later on he quizzed me about my reasons. I told him he should have brought me on because it might have lifted the crowd and that could have helped the team. To my surprise he admitted he'd never even thought of that. I knew my choice was the right one.

Mick has since told people that story isn't true. There is never a problem when we meet up, we get on well and I think he's done a great job for Wolves. But that is definitely the real version of events after the Iceland draw.

LEARNING SOME DRESSING ROOM TRUTHS

I learned a lot from every boss I worked with, even in my non-league days. At South Liverpool a guy called Russell Perkins was player-manager, a nice fella who was also a schoolteacher.

I played up front with him. He was shrewd and knew how to play the game. He'd always be diving or getting pushed over by centre-backs to win penalties.

Each manager has different methods. Len Ashurst had some strange ways of attempting to make us up our levels at Newport County.

"You've got a nice house now, you're not living in a house with an outside toilet in that shit-hole Garston place," he once said to me. When I told my dad about it he was going to come down to south Wales and give him a hiding.

Len thought I was getting carried away and just coasting along because I'd scored a few goals. The truth was I was playing on an injury. I had tendonitis.

In a way I can see where Len was coming from. He was trying to get a reaction, even if his way of going about it was a bit extreme. He certainly made me a better player. Len was a harsh taskmaster. He'd really come down on you and that was just what I needed when I was young. I remember scoring twice against Scunthorpe, despite the fact I hadn't played well. I said so in the dressing room afterwards and Len emphatically agreed with me. "Fucking damn right," he roared, "you should be playing a lot better."

After I moved on to Oxford I worked with the legendary Jim Smith. He was a funny bloke. When we played five-a-side on a Friday he'd join in, even though he couldn't run at all. His idea was simply to score more goals than the opposition. That's why we played with two wingers and two full-backs, Bobby McDonald and Dave Langan, who also just went forward whenever they had possession. The lads on the flanks got the ball in the box all the time. As a striker it was brilliant to be on the end of such great service.

Jim took us to the 1985 Second Division title, but didn't hang around much longer after that. Surprisingly he moved on to QPR after a contract disagreement with Robert Maxwell. We were all shocked and it meant Maurice Evans, already part of the coaching staff, would be the one to lead us in the First Division. As expected we struggled near the bottom, even if we did manage to go all the way in the League Cup and win it against QPR, managed by Jim Smith. Surprisingly though we managed to stay up, finishing in 18th place, a point above relegated Ipswich Town.

As much as survival was a relief it was apparent to all of us, and particularly Maurice, that 1986/87 would again be spent at the wrong end of the 22–team division.

An indifferent start, 21 points from our first 16 games,

rightly had us all in a bad mood. Maurice didn't deal with it too well, especially after a 1-1 draw at QPR. A few of us went for a badly needed drink and when we finished the team bus had disappeared.

They had left us in London and we needed a lift from some supporters to get us home. Maurice did apologise, explaining he'd been annoyed because we'd conceded a last minute goal to my Republic of Ireland team-mate John Byrne. He hadn't handled the situation in the best way, something I was guilty of myself on plenty of occasions when I became a manager.

CELTIC DREAM BUT THE MERSEY CALLS

Everton 0 Tranmere 3, FA Cup fourth round, 2001.

That was my best day as Tranmere boss. To win by such a margin at Goodison Park was fantastic. On the pitch at the end I remained very dignified and made sure I shook hands with everyone and clapped their fans. As soon as I got in the dressing room I started dancing and singing like a little kid.

Less than two months after that victory against Everton, I'd resigned.

I always thought the possibility of being a manager might come along one day, especially at Tranmere where I'd really enjoyed my time as a player. If the job ever came up I knew I'd give it a go and, in 1996, it did. I lasted five years in charge, mostly great years.

By then I'd been at the club since the summer of 1991. Moving from Sociedad back to England was the best decision for my family, even if not many clubs were willing to put their faith in a soon to be 33-year-old striker. In fact there was a major lack of First Division sides that thought I could do a job for them.

Surely my goalscoring record in Spain, and before I'd gone

there, showed what I could bring. Leeds United were mentioned and Howard Wilkinson had watched me play against Barcelona in the Nou Camp at the end of the 1990/91 season.

I scored twice that night against a team who were collecting the Championship trophy. Dalian also got on the scoresheet in our 3-1 victory. Somehow it wasn't enough to convince the Leeds boss of my value, though. When I was Tranmere manager some years later, I fell out with Wilkinson over his treatment of one of my players. It was when he was in charge of the England Under-21s. He called up our goalkeeper Steve Simonsen. Tranmere were playing on the Friday night but he wouldn't let Steve play for us because he was joining up with England on the Saturday. I couldn't see the sense in that when Steve needed as many games as possible for experience. We had a big row on the phone and I wanted to have a go at him about his decision not to make a move for me after that game at Barcelona, but in the end I chose not to.

Celtic were another of the sides I'd heard whispers about, although they never made any approach for me. When Ireland played against a Manchester United X1 in Matt Busby's testimonial at Old Trafford later that summer I got chatting to Liam Brady, my former international team-mate who had recently taken over as manager of the Glasgow side. "I didn't know you were looking for a move back from Spain," Chippy told me, "I'd have signed you in an instant."

For once I was speechless. I couldn't believe it; everyone in the game knew I wanted to come back to Britain. I would loved to have played for Celtic and not because I played for Ireland or because I'm Catholic.

The Lisbon Lions was the major draw for me. I still remember those 1967 legends really well and the fact they were all from the same small area of Glasgow and went on to win the European Cup. I loved the likes of Jimmy Johnstone and Bobby Lennox. After I'd retired it would have been great to say I'd played for Liverpool, the Republic of Ireland and Celtic. It didn't happen.

More importantly for my family, we were on our way back to Merseyside and Tranmere. Rovers were a club on the up having just been promoted to the old Second Division under Johnny King.

By the time I'd made my 287th – and final – appearance for the Wirral men in May 1998 my goal tally stood at an impressive 174. That included nine hat-tricks.

Johnny's belief in me, which nobody else possessed, had been rewarded. Johnny had tried to take me to Prenton Park during his first spell as boss there, when I was beginning my career at South Liverpool.

Rovers didn't have the couple of grand needed to get me and I went to Newport instead. He was a lovely fella, who rarely, if ever, lost the plot. I had the utmost respect for him. He actively encouraged us to go out together and was very into team spirit. He'd organise the Christmas party and ensure everyone joined in the festivities. He believed we should enjoy ourselves and also work hard, traditions that I tried to carry on when I became boss.

Those old fashioned ways were great when it came to building camaraderie. In other areas I felt we needed to change. Johnny had a habit of talking up the opposition before games. That was unusual and had an adverse affect on us sometimes. We'd be really concerned about what they were going to do, rather than focusing on our own efforts.

Aside from that, I enjoyed working with him and, for a time, the club appeared destined to step up to the Premier League. We were very unfortunate not to reach the League Cup final in 1994.

A goal from my mate Dalian Atkinson after a controversial

free-kick at the end of the semi-final first leg gave Aston Villa an undeserved consolation in an emphatic 3-1 defeat at Prenton Park. We really battered them and should have finished with a bigger lead. Villa won the second leg by the same scoreline before coming through a penalty shoot-out. We had also looked good for promotion in the 1990s only to mess it up on three occasions, losing out at the play-off semi-final stage each time. Liam O'Brien even had the chance to put us through to Wembley in one play-off but missed his penalty.

Three years in a row we lost in the play-off semi-finals. The most disappointing of those was in 1995. At one stage we only needed nine points from our last five league games to go up automatically. Somehow we didn't get them. After that failure it became obvious we would never do it.

MY BIG CHANCE

People have often asked me if I had a feeling that the manager's time in charge was coming to an end in April 1996. Some players might have felt that way, I didn't. We played Derby County at the Baseball Ground and lost 6-2 on a Bank Holiday Monday. They absolutely battered us and afterwards Chairman Frank Corfe wanted to make a change.

He spoke to the physio, Les Parry, who was very highly thought of at the club even back then. Les said if Johnny was going to go that I'd be the best person to step in. I wish it had been done in a different manner.

Basically Johnny was still in charge when I was offered his job and that was the wrong way to sort out the situation. I said I couldn't take the position behind anyone's back, especially someone I had so much time for.

The chairman told me it was going to Ronnie Moore, the assistant manager, if I didn't accept it. I felt bad but if I didn't commit I knew Ronnie would definitely have said yes. I wasn't a big fan of his because he would be critical of Johnny at times. Even though I didn't like the way it was all being carried out, I shook the chairman's hand and took the job.

We were playing Leicester the following day so trained as normal. Afterwards, Frank got everyone together and announced the change. "Fucking hell," was the reaction from most of the lads, followed by a long silence. I might have contemplated the move before, but it was still a shock for me too when it actually became a reality.

As it sunk in, the players seemed genuinely pleased by my appointment. That was confirmed when I suggested that anyone who didn't want to play for me should exit the room. Nobody did. Others on the staff weren't so enthused by the news. I told Ronnie Moore he was a goner. Kenny Jones, the kitman, would have been told the same, except for the fact that I couldn't find him. He never showed up again.

Of the staff that stayed my main message was: "If anyone says I'm wrong, you say I'm right." We were all in the situation together and had to be united. I told them they'd be sacked if they had been speaking out against me to others. I knew that certain people had been talking about Johnny behind his back and I thought that was wrong. I also said I was learning the job from scratch so I was going to get it wrong sometimes. I might make mistakes, but they'd be honest mistakes.

The players were all my mates. I said if they played well they'd be in the team, if they didn't they'd be out. There was no rotation; we never had enough good players for that.

I spoke to Johnny a lot afterwards. Him and his family were quite rightly hurt by how it ended at Tranmere. Unfortunately things like that happen in football all the time. The end comes for everyone.

MAKING A SPLASH

It was a new start and I took to the job pretty quickly, even if it felt like we were similar to Rag Arse Rovers at times.

I tried to introduce a few changes during my first pre-season as boss, although I realised there were some things I could do little about. Before the players returned to training I was in for a few days with Les Parry to ensure everything was ready for the 1996/97 season. One of the lads, I won't name any names, surprisingly turned up looking for treatment, saying he'd done his hamstring. I couldn't believe it. "Were you out playing football?" I asked him. "No, no," he sheepishly said. "Out for a run?" "No, nothing like that," he replied again with an embarrassed look on his face.

Finally he explained the circumstances. "I was having a bath last night with my missus. We were having a bit of fun and I managed to pull my hamstring."

It must be one of the most pleasant ways to get injured I told him. There was little else I could say apart from laugh at the circumstances.

In that pre-season I also tried to introduce a course of weight training for some of the younger lads, to build them up. It took place twice a week in the gym. I joined in and so did some of the senior players. A lot of them had never used weights before and we did a real tough workout to get them started.

When they came in again they were all joking about how sore and stiff they had been after the first session. Alan Morgan said: "Boss I couldn't even wipe my arse the next morning because I was so stiff." Everyone was cracking up with laughter when Alan Rogers shouted: "You think that was bad, I was driving towards a big roundabout and my arms were so stiff I couldn't turn the steering wheel. I ended up going straight through the middle of the roundabout."

'PASSION, COMMITMENT, DESIRE AND MADNESS'
Prior to me taking charge there had been no dietary advice and we usually had a few beers the night before away matches. I tried to change that. Giving instructions was something I found frustrating. At the top level a player only needs to be told something once. Lower down they need to hear it a million times.

When we were playing Port Vale I wanted Gareth Roberts to stop their dangerous winger getting the ball in to the box. I told him that was his only job and he did it very well. In our very next game crosses from Gareth's side were flying in all afternoon, there were so many you would have needed to be wearing a crash helmet. It was because I'd never told him to cut out the supply again; he didn't know what to do.

After a while I started writing down instructions for the team and gave everyone specific jobs. The lads must have been sick of hearing the same thing over and over. I certainly got tired of saying it.

My real forte was motivation. My strong point was getting in players' heads. I'd throw cups, I'd swear, I'd scream, whatever it took. At times it had spectacular effects, such as the night we recovered from being 3-0 down at half-time against Southampton in the cup to win 4-3.

Southampton were well in control at the interval but as we were going back to the dressing room I saw something that made my blood boil. Glenn Hoddle and his assistant John Gorman were giving each other high fives. They thought the game was won. Kevin Sheedy said to me: "Look at them – they think it's over". That proved the perfect motivation for a great comeback. I'd never really got on with Glenn Hoddle as a person so that result was extra sweet. We were also losing 2-0 against David O'Leary's Leeds in the League Cup and managed to turn it around to win 3-2.

When you are outside the Premier League being able to do that and get something extra from individuals can make all the difference. Graham Taylor told me it was one of the key factors in his Watford side gaining promotion to the top division through the play-offs in 1998/99. They put together a fantastic run at the end of the season, not losing in any of their last 10 league games. One of those came against us in a really tough battle where a couple of players were sent off.

Both sides fought all the way. Afterwards Graham told me he'd brought in an Irish sports psychologist to give his lads a boost.

This guy arrived in one day and told the players to shut up and watch a video he was about to put on. Within minutes they were shaking their head in disbelief. "It's a bunch of crazy Irish men running around with sticks battering each other," was their verdict on what they'd just watched. It had been a game of hurling.

The psychologist asked what qualities the hurlers had displayed. "Passion, commitment, desire and madness," the players replied. "Unpaid," the psychologist wrote on the board as he explained that hurlers were amateurs and didn't get a penny for their efforts. Graham reckoned watching that video obviously helped the Watford players draw even more from themselves and eventually contributed to them going up.

Getting into the Premier League was something we never achieved, even though we defeated plenty of the teams from the division above us.

I got the better of a lot of decent managers such as Peter Reid at Sunderland, David O'Leary at Leeds United, Bryan Robson at Middlesbrough, Hoddle, Gordon Strachan at Coventry, Walter Smith at Everton and Harry Redknapp at West Ham. They are all high profile names.

THE MEDAL THAT WAS HARDEST TO EARN

In 2000 we even reached Wembley. It was a proud moment for me to walk out alongside Martin O'Neill for the League Cup final. Tranmere had never been to a major final before and, despite our cup success, not many people would have predicted we'd go so far. As we came out of the tunnel I was emotional.

My dad had died two years earlier and prior to then he'd attended every game at Wembley where I'd been involved. I thought of him again at that moment. I also looked around at the 29,000 Rovers fans and that made me very proud.

It was a new experience for them, the players too and me as a boss. In my playing days I'd always just focussed on getting my own game right ahead of a big occasion. Now I had to worry about everyone else.

My main priority was getting the lads to relax. We took them down to London on the Thursday to let them enjoy it all. Going up against Martin was a big test for me. I've got the utmost respect for him; he's a real football man and a nice bloke too. I don't think he was too happy that I slapped Theodoros Zagorakis, as I've already discussed. But I explained my reasons afterwards and I think he knew where I was coming from. Martin is very similar to me in that he shows his passion all the time and he's done a few silly things on the sidelines too.

I knew it was going to be hard with the game taking place at Wembley. If it had been at Prenton Park we would have fancied our chances. We did our homework and tried to find ways to nullify how Leicester played.

Setpieces were a big threat, especially when it came to Matt Elliott at corners. The sending off of Clint Hill cost us in the end.

Because we were down to ten men we didn't have someone on the post and that's where the ball went in. Normally we would have had someone in that position. I felt Clint was a little bit unfortunate to be dismissed; Emile Heskey went down like a sack of spuds... as usual.

Even then we still got back in the contest through David Kelly, before losing 2-1. Afterward I told the lads not to be disappointed. They'd reached a Wembley Cup final and had to build on that.

It had to be their ambition to get there again. The medal I got as manager is one of the best I've won. It was harder earned than any of the others.

As a player you play because you have some natural skills, as a manager you have to do everything and it doesn't come easily.

'HEY YOU... SORRY ABOUT GEORGE!'

No matter whether we won or lost we always provided entertainment for the fans at Tranmere, even if some people at the FA wouldn't have approved of what was on show. One of the more forgettable moments occurred in pre-season – thankfully – when not too many people were watching. It involved George Santos, a lovely guy who we bought from Toulon in France. Most of the time he was a gentle giant but on the pitch you didn't mess with him. Somebody should have told Paul Dickov this before we played Manchester City.

I always liked Dickov and the way he put himself about on the pitch. On this occasion he tangled with George who appeared to head-butt him. Dickov went down and Santos was sent off. Les Parry was beside me in the dugout and he insisted George was innocent. When George got near the sideline we asked him about what happened and he said: "I didn't touch him."

I was livid as I spotted Dickov being substituted for his own good by Joe Royle. This is my chance to have a go at him I thought to myself.

"Hey you," I started, and I was about to scream every name under the sun at him when he turned around and had this huge lump on his head. It was like something from a Tom and Jerry cartoon. "I'm sorry about George Santos," I said as I tried not to laugh.

We could never criticise the lads for misbehaving too much, Kevin Sheedy and me were just as bad. In every game we always had a go at the linesman on our side of the pitch and tried to intimidate him.

Against Bury we were at it again when their boss, Stan Ternent, had enough of us. Stan's a tough character and not someone you mess with. "Are you letting these two run this game or are you going to do it yourself?" he shouted at the linesman. "Fuck off," I said and squirted a water bottle right in Stan's face, into his mouth. He was seething and spat his chewing gum out. We pissed ourselves laughing. Those were

My team: Tranmere v Liverpool at my testimonial (above) and in Real Sociedad kit with son Paul (left), Kevin Richardson in the background. Right: The next generation – my grandson Jamie proudly wearing his Liverpool kit and me at home (top)

Honour: With the Merseyside Sports Personality of the Year trophy. Donning Beatles wigs with former team-mates (below) at an Anfield reunion and (right), I didn't make a habit of this – dressed as a nun on a night out with Newport County...

Heading through: My goal against Mexico (top) at USA '94 proved crucial. Above: Celebrating another strike with my mate Kevin Sheedy

Gone fishing: One of the best ways to wind down away from football

Off to a flier: Scoring at Highbury, 1987

Above: Lifted shoulder high by the fans at the airport in Istanbul; at a sportsmen's dinner with big Jack; sharing a joke with my mate Peter Reid during an interview and Irish dancing for TV show 'A Question Of Sport'

Home: In the Anfield dressing room. Above: With two massive heroes of mine – Kop striking legends Roger Hunt and Ian St John

Meet the boss: Behind the manager's desk at Prenton Park

Goodbye: Thumbs up to the Tranmere fans after my final game as a player in 1998

Silverware: Going head to head with Martin O'Neill for the Worthington Cup at Wembley in 2000 and (left) holding 'Ol' Big Ears' after Istanbul

Always on my mind: Laying a wreath at the Hillsborough memorial at Anfield and (top) speaking at the 20th anniversary service in 2009

For the fans: A goal with my first touch against Everton in the 1989 FA Cup final

Never again: Singing on TV in Ireland was nerve-wracking – even though I ended up winning the competition!
Top: In my 'Aldo's Place' bar in Liverpool a couple of years ago

I'm back: Wearing the number 8 shirt and scoring again in front of the Kop

the kind of antics I used to get up to on the sideline. That's why I think I never got offered any big job. If I'm being honest I probably needed someone to advise me and guide me. Sheeds was my mate and he was 100 per cent behind me, I probably needed someone to manage me.

LOSING ALAN WAS BEGINNING OF THE END

Losing Alan Mahon convinced me we'd never be successful and it also damaged a long-standing friendship I'd had with my former international team-mate Kevin Moran.

Alan, a Dubliner, was one of our most talented young players. If we had got decent money for him his departure wouldn't have been so bad. Instead we got nothing. Alan was very important in our system at Tranmere, he played on the left side of the midfield three. If you were stuck he might play on the wing too.

In 1999 his contract was running out and he told me he was going to speak to some agents in London. I told him not to do that, I'd sort something for him. I went to Kevin, who was working with Paul Stretford, and asked him to look after Alan because they were friends. I didn't want anything from it, unlike a lot of other managers.

They all met and I said to Paul all I wanted was for the lad to sign a contract with Rovers. That was around October time. When the following March or April came along they told me he wouldn't be signing. I was fuming. Paul told me they'd get us a decent fee for him to buy a replacement. To cut a long story short they took him to Sporting Lisbon on a free transfer. I rang Stretford and told him what I thought of him. I felt he had stabbed me in the back. I also believed Kevin should have done better. He'd obviously sided with the agent. I used to always get on very well with Kevin. Our friendship is not what it was after what happened.

Trying to get someone to replace Alan was impossible. He had been one of our best players at that time and the team wasn't the same without him. We couldn't build anything for the long term. It was just one short-term solution after another when it came to bringing in new faces. In that situation you're barely keeping the club alive and you realise it can't go on that way forever. You start to go backwards. It got to the point where I couldn't continue and ended up quitting on March 17, 2001, St. Patrick's Day. We were 2-0 up against Barnsley at half-time and absolutely battered them but ended up losing 3-2.

I was worn down by it all and had to leave. There was too much wrong at the club for us to ever do well.

LORRAINE KNEW WHAT SHE WANTED

Even Lorraine Rogers would agree with me on that. I've got tremendous respect for the woman who took over the role of chairwoman in 1999.

She was hard to work for and very demanding, traits I'd expect from a person in that position. The club always seemed to be running at a big loss and because of that she'd want to chat to me about different details every day. Sometimes I had to sneak out to make sure she wouldn't see me leaving the stadium.

She eventually got to grips with everything that was going on and put Rovers back on its feet. We got to the stage where we actually weren't losing money. Player sales were still necessary, though, to keep us afloat.

I never wanted to lose any of my lads. The only player I felt we should transfer was Jason Koumas in 2000/01. I once spotted a fax that wasn't meant for me from Ron Noades at Crystal Palace who was bidding £2m for Jason. He was a good lad, very talented and definitely had lots of natural flair. He'd been at Liverpool as a youngster and his ability to run with the ball was fantastic. Manchester United and other Premier League teams had watched him very closely. But his potential was accompanied by flaws. He should have been stronger mentally and I tried to get more effort from him.

On a Monday morning, after I'd been out on the beer the

day before, I'd challenge him to come ahead of me in the running we did to warm up. I'd threaten him with extra running after training if he finished behind me. It didn't matter what I said, he'd still end up last. It was so frustrating for all of us.

I felt the offer from Palace was too good to turn down. I told Lorraine I didn't even want all of the money, we could have spent just £800,000 of it on a few players and that would have been enough to stave off relegation. She disagreed and felt we'd eventually get £4m for Jason from someone. I said that would never happen, that he'd reached his highest value and we should sell while that was the case.

In 2002 they did transfer him, to West Brom for £2.2m. The fact that the people above me at the club felt they knew more about a player's worth than me was another reason for believing the end was approaching. My choice was the right one.

BARNESIE, LES AND A ROVERS RETURN?

I could have gone back to Prenton Park a few years later, before Ronnie Moore took over. I went and spoke to Lorraine. Jason McAteer had been on at me to give it another go. The plan was for him to do the coaching and I'd be the manager. They put a good contract in front of me and I initially thought I'd take it. I slept on it. When I woke up I changed my mind. I didn't feel it was right. The club didn't have any money to spend and it would have been very difficult to get anywhere. I suffered because of that the first time around and I didn't want to experience the same again.

Now I want them to get back up the league despite my time there concluding in a sour way. The club didn't even give me a full month's wage; they only paid me up until the day I left. As I've already said, that angered me.

I was there for ten years, longer than any other club. I have loads of time for the fans and I have been back a few times to watch them play. I never thought Les Parry was management material if I'm honest but I'd love to see him do well.

Barnesie lost it a little when he became boss in 2009 because he tried to play total football. You can't do it in that division. The wage bill had just been reduced and he didn't have the quality of players needed to play that style. Confidence in the team disappeared and it was sad to see it go that way. I really wanted it to work for the lads because I'm fond of Tranmere, and Barnesie and Jason are my mates. Les tried to rebuild the fighting spirit when he took over and managed to stay up. He did a good job.

Since I was last a manager I've had offers from a few other clubs too, including Oxford United on more than one occasion. I admit the thought of going there did appeal to me. I really enjoyed my time with the club and the fans voted me their best ever player.

I met with the owner, Firoz Kassam, a few times and he offered me good terms to take charge, especially for a non-league team. Thankfully I'd done some enquiries and knew the club was having a lot of trouble and the supporters had turned against him. I got the impression he wanted me there to appease the fans and take the heat off him. Appointing me would have bought him some time.

THE IRELAND JOB

A position I would certainly have taken in the past was Ireland manager. Looking back at it now I felt, rightly or wrongly, that they'd made their decision before we all went to Dublin for the interviews when I first applied for the job in 2002. I'd had some time out of the game after Tranmere and was ready to get back into it all again.

Mick McCarthy had quit after a poor start to the qualifying campaign for the 2004 Euros and I sent the FAI my CV. When we sat down with them I honestly thought I was the favourite. I explained exactly what I'd done at Tranmere by bringing in so much money from the cup runs and they were definitely impressed by that. I also told them about the managers I'd got the better of. Some of those names were on the shortlist for the job, guys like Peter Reid and Bryan Robson. Frank Stapleton, Joe Kinnear and Philippe Troussier were also supposedly in contention.

A lot of people say now that it was going to be Brian Kerr who got it, no matter what. The decision was a joke, a terrible choice. I'd met Brian once while I was over in Dublin working at a game. After we'd spoken I thought it was him who had played for Ireland 69 times, not me. He came across as very, very arrogant.

When he was in charge he seemed very wary of ex-players working in the media. I thought he was very fortunate to get the position. It's one thing managing the U16s and U18s. He did very well at that level. When you're in charge of professionals who are on twenty and thirty grand a week, or even more, it's very different. He had some decent results, but mainly in friendlies. When he needed to win important qualifying games he didn't do it. He'd never dealt with those situations at the top level and couldn't handle it.

I went for the job again in 2006, when Steve Staunton got it. An agent here in Liverpool, Dave Lockwood, got in touch with the FAI for me. He said I'd be meeting with them in late January. Two weeks before that was due to take place it was announced that Stan had got it. The FAI said they never had a conversation with an agent on my behalf.

Stan is a great friend of mine. But I thought the FAI took a big risk putting him in that position. He didn't have enough experience to become an international boss. Dealing with the media is a major part of it and he's probably too honest for his own good when it comes to that side of the game. Journalists took advantage of his honesty and really went for him. He didn't deserve that, nobody who has served their country so well does. After what I'd gone through at Tranmere I think would have been better prepared for it all.

EX-PLAYERS CAN HELP THE BOSS

One area that I think is vitally important for managers to be in control of is scouting.

Ireland always do their homework when it comes to scouting for players who can represent the country, such as lads like Ray Houghton and myself.

At Liverpool that area of the club has some massive question marks against it in recent times. It's a vital part of the game and you have to say those at Anfield haven't always been getting it right in recent years.

The number of players who have come and gone is unbelievable. And the amount of those who clearly haven't been good enough from the first day is also alarming.

I'm talking about the likes of Salif Diao, Antonio Nunez, Bruno Cheyrou, Phillip Degen and Nabil El Zhar. Sometimes you can see foreign players have talent but can't adapt to the physical side of the English game. Alberto Aquilani might be one of those. But nobody can tell me the likes of Voronin or Degen are talented.

The scout who recommended them got it wrong, although it's not just the scout's fault. The manager should go and try to watch these players too. David Moyes does that a lot, so should any Liverpool boss. Watching tapes or DVDs isn't enough. You only see the good parts on those, any agent can edit the footage together.

I think that former players have an important role to play in this area. My idea, moving forward, would be for scouts to focus on different regions around the world. I would use former players to do this so that they can be there to talent spot the best 10, 11, 12, 13, 14 and 15-year-olds and bring them to the club. I could be an ambassador for Portugal, a country I know well, Jan could look after Denmark, Glenn Hysen Sweden and so on.

The ex-Liverpool players are football people through and through, who know about the game. So many of them work in the media now but they could be utilised by Liverpool in this way. I would be proud to work for the club in this capacity.

Of course, one issue is finding the funding to employ all these scouts but many would do it for the love of the club anyway or perhaps they would only be rewarded when they uncovered a real starlet. That would be a good incentive for the ex-pros. If one of us uncovers the next Ronaldo or Torres it would be well worth it.

They'd be motivated by the fact that they'd be helping to rebuild Liverpool. If I was given that responsibility, I'll be honest, I'd be thrilled.

I'd go out there and leave no stone unturned in my efforts to find the next Steven Gerrard. And if they made it to the first team I'd be absolutely delighted.

You do wonder what drives some scouts. There are a lot of players recommended to clubs and it can't be based on talent. Something else must be influencing them.

A key strength that always used to put Liverpool ahead of the rest when it came to recruitment was being able to spot if a player was on the way down, and get a replacement in before he completely lost it.

They were better at that than anyone else in Europe. Now they never do that.

It's not an easy task, but for example who is going to replace Steven Gerrard and Jamie Carragher?

They will be absolutely massive losses when they finish playing for the club.

MANAGERS DURING MY CAREER
1. Len Ashurst (Newport County)
2. Colin Addison (Newport County)
3. Jim Smith (Oxford United)
4. Kenny Dalglish (Liverpool)
5. Marco Boronat (Sociedad)
6. John Toshack (Sociedad)
7. John King (Tranmere Rovers)
8. Jack Charlton (Ireland)

8 CUP SHOCKS CAUSED BY TRANMERE

1. Coventry City (League Cup)
2. Middlesbrough (League Cup)
3. West Ham United (FA Cup)
4. Sunderland (FA Cup)
5. Leeds United (League Cup)
6. Fulham (FA Cup) – Fulham were in the same division as us but nobody expected us to go to their place and win
7. Everton (FA Cup)
8. Southampton (FA Cup)

PLAYING THE GAME

'They think it's Ald over... it is now!'

'Irish soccer hero John Aldridge last night reached the goal of Charity You're a Star champ.

'The 47-year-old admitted he can't sing a note but still managed to steal the viewers' hearts and win the national TV singing competition.

'Pop guru Louis Walsh said Aldo could even get to number one in Ireland now...'

Daily Mirror, August 2006

Never thought I'd make the front page of Angler's Mail – or the Mirror for singing...

NOT HAVING THE X-FACTOR

Playing football, scoring goals, taking penalties, talking on the radio, it's all easy compared to singing live on TV. It was so scary I can't go near a karaoke machine any longer. I'm even afraid to hum along to a tune on the radio now. For a start I can't sing, which obviously makes the task even harder.

Somehow those nerves and my inability to hit a note didn't prevent me winning Charity You're A Star on Irish TV in 2006.

The Irish equivalent of The X-Factor was an event to raise money for good causes and featured various celebrities from radio and TV, plus me. I'd taken part in plenty of golf events to raise money for Temple Street Children's Hospital in Dublin and never had a problem doing that. When I was asked to enter the singing competition for the same cause I initially refused. "I can't sing," I honestly told the organisers. They refused to take no for an answer and kept ringing, texting and emailing me. "Just have a go and if you're rubbish it's not a problem," they reasoned with me.

After weeks of this I eventually agreed to take part. Even now I get chills when I think about it. Apart from the obvious problem, of not being able to sing, I didn't know the exact details of the show either. I thought it was going to be pre-recorded on just a single day. Nearly two weeks later I was still involved.

Somehow I managed to muddle through the early rounds and from there people kept voting for me. It was similar to the situation with John Sergeant on Dancing On Ice. He was rubbish and everyone loved him. His awful dancing ability was better than my singing, but again, though, everyone seemed to like me.

That was despite the fact I even forgot the words a couple of times, most embarrassingly during Ring of Fire. Instead of singing I just chanted 'der der-der der-der der der derrrrr', looked a right idiot and tried not to laugh. After that I told the organisers we all needed a screen with the words on it to help us. Thankfully they introduced that to the show. Something else that helped me was having a drink beforehand. We were told not to, but I was shaking so much I always needed a few glasses of wine to calm me down.

Four days into the competition I had to go back to Liverpool because it was driving me crazy. Another problem was I'd run out of songs because I only know about two.

"I can't do it any more," I told Joan, "I can't go back." She advised me to have a look at the jukebox in the house and pick out a few tunes that I liked. I also had none other than Louis Walsh guiding me, believe it or not. He wanted me to perform some Kenny Rogers numbers. It didn't matter what advice he provided, I just had a terrible voice.

Somehow I managed to win the final and raised about 160,000 euro. I even recorded Ring Of Fire and Lily The Pink for a CD that helped bring in a few more quid too. When it was all done I had a huge glass of wine. It was a massive relief to get it over with.

Afterwards I went to see the kids in the hospital and I knew it had been worth all the effort. Ever since Hillsborough I've always found situations like that very difficult. In the ward I had a big lump in my throat and was almost in tears. It showed that what I'd gone through was nothing really.

But I'm still certain I won't be singing on live television ever again.

GOLF PUNK

Apart from disastrous attempts at singing, and working in the media, a lot of my time is now spent on the golf course. You'd imagine that someone with my temperament wouldn't have the calmness required to enjoy 18 holes.

At first that was the case, and I can still remember chucking a club into a ditch with such force that I couldn't find it afterwards. I was playing with Steve Hothersall and his brother, who I'd only just met. Steve's brother quite rightly thought I was a nutcase. I used to be terrible for throwing clubs around when I got frustrated, but thankfully I'm not so bad now.

My temper was once my problem out on the course; with Jason McAteer it's his etiquette, or lack of it. Jason is a super player – it's just a pity he doesn't behave properly.

The worst example came at a pro-am competition in Portugal. The prize for the winner was about 15,000 euro and the guy we were playing alongside was still in contention. Jason was putting first and the ball lipped out of the hole. Instead of tapping it in from a few centimetres away, picking it up and getting out of the way he decided to practice the putt again. While he was going through his routine the lad with us had been lining up his shot, to win. Jason walked right across him and the guy quite rightly went nuts.

That came straight after another incident on the 17th hole when the pro's shot went in the water. Naturally he was pretty worried about it and was looking at his options. In the meantime, Jason was in trouble too.

Instead of letting the guy get on with his own game Jason started screaming: "What do I do with this? What would you do?" He wanted the pro to go over and look at his ball. I'm sure that was the last of his concerns. If there was no cash involved he would have been perfectly within his rights to have a go at Jason, the fact that 15,000 euro was resting on it meant he could have whacked him with his club and not felt bad.

Usually when we play the stakes aren't so high, we can have a laugh because it's for charity. A lot of the lads from the LFC former players association take part in tournaments to raise money for good causes and we get names from other sports and celebrities to join in too. Sue Griffiths at Liverpool helps us organise those days out and they're always entertaining.

When it comes to players' handicaps quite a few of the lads over-exaggerate, with myself, Alan Kennedy and John Durnin probably being the worst. I'm on 16 at the moment and I'm looking to reduce it further. Gary Gillespie is a fantastic player and Ronnie Whelan has got himself down to a low handicap too.

It's a surprise some of the lads still take the risk of playing now because when I was at Liverpool Steve McMahon was struck by lightning while out on the course. Everyone found it frightening... but quite amusing too.

JACK'S A SORE LOSER

Golf has taken over from fishing as one of my main passions now. In the past I never thought that would happen.

I still love fishing and do so whenever I go to my villa in Portugal. I've got loads of friends in Praia Da Luz. If Ireland is my country and Liverpool is my city, then Praia Da Luz is my village, it really is a home from home and I spend as much time there as possible. It was a tragedy when Madeleine McCann disappeared in that part of what is a beautiful area. It's not that sort of place and my heart went out to her family. Hopefully she will one day be found.

Whenever I go fishing in Portugal it's usually with my friends from the Cave Bar. We catch a few fish, usually carp, and have a laugh. It's never really competitive, unlike the occasion when I went fly fishing with Jack Charlton.

Within an hour or two I'd caught a few more trout than him. Jack being Jack, he said he was moving further along the river. I stayed in my spot and continued to reel them in. When we eventually decided to call it a day my net was full. Jack informed me that he'd caught a lot more but put them all back. I had to smile when I heard that.

Any time I do come home with a good catch I'll try to cook it for dinner. I've always loved getting into the kitchen and preparing a meal. During my time as manager at Tranmere I found it was the only way I could get football off my mind. Otherwise I'd be thinking about it all the time.

I'll attempt to make anything but curries are my favourite.

Joan tells me I'm a great cook, maybe she only says that though so she doesn't have to do it.

I even watch cookery shows to pick up tips. That first started when I finished with Tranmere in 2001. I still wanted to keep myself in shape and went running on the treadmill every day. I'd be running and watching Ready Steady Cook on the TV – how sad is that!

'THAT'S FIVE EUROPEAN CUPS, FERGIE…'

If I'm not working, golfing or cooking I sometimes do after-dinner speaking. It's usually an enjoyable experience, especially when it gave me the chance to take the piss out of Sir Alex Ferguson.

The PFA had asked me to give a speech at the 2007 PFA awards in London. Naturally, I said yes. When I got there the room was full with about 2,000 people, including all the FA, UEFA and FIFA dignitaries. Fergie was sitting three seats away from me, with Bobby Charlton and Brian Barwick also nearby.

What a great opportunity to have a little dig at Fergie I thought to myself, as I looked around the intimidating crowd. My set went on for about 20 minutes, and I talked about the Liverpool team that I played for and the history of the club. I mentioned how talented the late eighties side were and the fact that we could have won the European Cup a few times if we hadn't been barred from Europe because of Heysel. Had we taken part, I declared, we'd now have won seven or eight European Cups instead of the FIVE Liverpool have.

As I said it, I held up my five fingers and said 'FIVE' again in the direction of Fergie. He just put his head down and didn't say anything. Brian Barwick, a well-known Liverpool fan, winked at me and laughed.

Later on that evening Fergie picked up an award and made a speech. He said his only regret was the fact he'd won just one European Cup, at that time. He said great teams like AC Milan have won it seven times and Real Madrid have won it loads, and Liverpool have won it four times. Not many people seemed to notice that he'd forgotten all about Istanbul. He was getting me back and did it with great style too. I had to say 'well done'.

Whenever I meet Fergie I get on fine with him. I think if he was Liverpool boss we'd love him, what he's done at United is similar to Shanks. My obsession was scoring goals, his is hating Liverpool and he's used that to make Manchester United successful. He looks after himself and he's very sharp mentally so I see him going on for a long time yet.

THE OLD BOYS

Naturally I'm not the only ex-Red who does some after-dinner work. It's always an enjoyable evening for everyone with some brilliant stories being told. My favourite involves Jason again.

As he was walking out of a club in Dublin one night he spotted Jimmy White sitting in the corner. Jason's a big fan of snooker so he shouts: "Jimmy." Jimmy turns around and waves at him.

Jason has had a few beers and gets muddled up.
He shouts back: "180."
The worst thing about it was Jason obviously knew who he was.
His brain just couldn't work fast enough.

Us ex-players always get together on a regular basis and we even play football now and again in the Masters Tournament. We have a decent side, even if our stamina isn't what it used to be. Jan Molby has lost it completely in terms of fitness, if he ever had it. He just can't move. But if you give him the ball he's a genius.

Phil Neal has two plastic hips and he's still brilliant. Alan Kennedy isn't quite with it any more but he still plays. Gary Gillespie, Barnesie, Jimmy Case and David Fairclough have a go too. Warky (John Wark) is great; he was still playing Sunday League not so long ago. We got some fresh legs into the side recently too. Jason, Phil Babb, Don Hutchison and Marshy do the running now, they're all fit, or fitter than us anyway. None of us are as good as we used to be, but we don't care because we enjoy it and enjoy each other's company.

NEVER FORGET YOUR ROOTS

Another side to being a former player is you get asked to give your support to various charities or good causes, as well as putting your name to different business ventures or projects where people think they can benefit from the publicity that being associated with a familiar face can bring.

Over recent years I've been involved in some interesting events. To name but a few, I've handed out awards at the ECHO Arena for the Liverpool Echo; played in a celebrity poker tournament (this time I didn't lose any money); been involved in a fun boxing match with ex-Manchester United player Clayton Blackmore (I won on points!); opened the new city centre store for Liverpool FC and was delighted to support an £8m project to redevelop Garston.

One of the more unusual events I was invited to was a Father Ted festival on the Aran Islands, off the west coast of Ireland. There were various themed activities associated with the hit comedy series. I travelled there with Tony Cascarino but the crossing was a bit rough to say the least. Cas looked as white as a sheet when he finally got off the boat. Another different experience was appearing on the TV sports quiz A Question Of Sport. I didn't appear as a panellist but as the mystery personality – doing a spot of Irish dancing.

Of course, I'm more than happy to give my support to worthy causes and charity events. It may be handing out awards for a local football club or raising funds for Hillsborough. Your roots are important. You never forget where you are from and I've never done that. You should help out whenever you can. Liverpool has always been important and if I can help out the city in any small way I can, then I will. The same goes for Ireland.

10 YEARS AND COUNTING...

Working for the media plays a part in these opportunities coming along. That brings us back to where we started.

I was told recently that I will soon celebrate 10 years as a pundit, dating back to the UEFA Cup of 2001 when I took my first steps on the road as a full-time member of the press by covering that amazing game in Dortmund.

There's no question what the biggest footballing high of the last 10 years has been in that time... Istanbul. Stevie's last gasp equalising goal at Cardiff in the 2006 FA Cup final was also sensational. We were going nowhere, the game was over as far as I was concerned. Only Stevie Gerrard could do that.

As for the low – then it has to be the 2009/10 campaign for Liverpool – that was hard to take. Athens in 2007 was disappointing but to a certain extent you can handle being beaten in a Cup final. We were better than them on the night and I just think Rafa got his tactics a bit wrong. Peter Crouch should have come on earlier than he did and we probably showed AC Milan too much respect.

I've learned an awful lot about the Premier League over the last decade. Obviously, when you're a lower league manager, like I was at Tranmere, the only Premier League football you see is on Match of the Day or certain other games. Through being involved with the media, I've learned loads about how players handle themselves, tactics and the way teams play. You become a little bit like a Chief Scout – I've already explained how I think former players like me can play an important role for the club in the future.

The game of football itself has changed massively over the past ten years. The cheating now that sometimes goes on, I can't stress too much, is simply unacceptable. The diving and trying to con the referee has stepped up to another level.

It's also disappointing to see smaller clubs continue to struggle for survival. As someone who worked his way up through the leagues, I would have liked to have seen money generated by the Football League from the bigger clubs. We've been saying for years that smaller clubs are struggling for finance and aren't bringing the grassroots players through. That should be happening more.

So what does the next ten years hold for Liverpool and Ireland?

There's more belief among the Irish people now. We came so close to qualifying for the World Cup, only to get cheated out of it. It seems there's optimism among the fans and some good young players coming through. We're not going to reach any semi-finals or finals for some years to come – but there is hope.

As for Liverpool, although I think we've got better players than we had a decade ago, I think the club has stagnated and we need to move on. We have to compete with the big clubs. We have to get 60,000 fans in Anfield for every game.

I think we will do it, we will get there. The commercial department at Liverpool, under Commercial Director Ian Ayre, has started to move the club forward but we need to make more progress in all areas. On the pitch, it sometimes feels like we're no closer to the likes of Chelsea and Manchester United than we were in 2001.

It would be nice if we finally see a new stadium in Stanley Park and we get back to where we were all those years ago. They say football success goes in cycles, so why can't we get back to where we were in the 1980s when I was playing?

That's the hope.

It would also be great if in ten years all the clubs were owned by the fans. It seems highly unlikely but you never know. Then perhaps football can get back to being a game for the working class man.

Whatever happens, what is certain is that the history and passion of Liverpool Football Club hasn't changed. That still counts for a lot. Who knows what will happen over the next decade. It is certainly going to be fascinating to see it all unfold. That's a journey for another day.

8 SONGS THAT HELPED ME WIN 'YOU'RE A STAR'
(Songs I picked for the competition)
1. Ring Of Fire – Johnny Cash
2. You're Sixteen – Ringo Starr
3. My First, My Last, My Everything – Barry White
4. Sweet Caroline – Neil Diamond
5. Little Ole Wine Drinker Me – Dean Martin
6. Most Beautiful Girl in the World – Charlie Rich
7. Rockin' All Over The World – Status Quo
8. Lilly The Pink – The Scaffold

FAVOURITE MUSICIANS
1. Luther Vandross
2. Elton John
3. U2
4. The Beatles
5. Johnny Cash
6. Lionel Richie
7. Barry White
8. Gerry Marsden (for THAT song)

FAVOURITE HOLIDAY DESTINATIONS
1. Praia Da Luz (Portugal)
2. Anywhere in Ireland
3. San Sebastian, Spain
4. Clear Water, Florida
5. Minorca
6. Majorca
7. Vilamoura (Portugal)
8. Mauritius

MY HEROES AWAY FROM FOOTBALL
(Only two)
1. Muhammad Ali
2. Ian Botham

THE BEST FORMER LFC PLAYERS AT GOLF

(In order of best first, in my opinion)

1. Alan Hansen
2. Gary Gillespie
3. Kenny Dalglish
4. Gary McAllister
5. John Durnin
6. Ronnie Whelan
7. Bruce Grobbelaar
8. Jason McAteer

8 PEOPLE I'VE PLAYED GOLF WITH

1. Alan Kennedy
2. Franny Norton (the jockey)
3. Don Hutchison
4. Nigel Spackman
5. Kieran Fallon (another jockey)
6. John Bishop (fantastic lad and what a great comedian.
He turned up at one of our golf days one Saturday and he was
superb – so funny)
7. Stan Boardman (Stan says the best club in his bag is the
'leather flipper'... in other words his golf shoe, which he uses to
flick the ball out of the rough when nobody is looking)
8. Mike Dean (the referee – during the round at Formby Hall,
he pulled the card out of his pocket another 18 times. For a
change it wasn't red or yellow – this time he was just
marking it!)

CHAPTER 13: MISCELLANEOUS

EXTRA TIME

Name: John Aldridge
Born: Liverpool
Car: Mercedes
Favourite meals: Curries, pasta and Chinese (come to think of it everything)
Favourite drink: Lager, water
Favourite ground: Nou Camp
Biggest attendance played before: 100,000
Most famous person met through football: The Pope with the Ireland squad in Rome, 1990

- Excerpts from the 'Aldo Factfile' from John Aldridge testimonial programme, 1996

I've kept the card from my
best ever round of golf...

Q & A

(Random questions put forward by fans)

Who was the worst dressed footballer you've known?

Nico (Stevie Nicol). He just didn't care what he wore.

Which footballer has had the flashiest car?

Probably Rushie had the best. He had a top of the range BMW. We all had decent cars at Liverpool, though.

Do you think the Aldo penalty shuffle should be allowed or were they right to ban it?

Should be allowed without a doubt. Whatever happens before the ball is kicked shouldn't be a problem should it? I can't see how it makes a difference.

Why didn't Bob Paisley get a knighthood?

I know they give them out a lot more freely these days but even so it wasn't right that he didn't get one for all he did for football. If Alex Ferguson has got one then Paisley should have.

You used to stay behind and take shots at Peter Beardsley when you were at Liverpool. Was he a good goalkeeper?

Alright, yeah – half decent. Obviously you could chip him – he wasn't the biggest! I used to dink it over him a few times.

Who had the worst haircut of all the players you've known?

Barnesie. He cut his hair once before we played Everton in the FA Cup at Goodison (the fifth round tie in February 1988) when Ray Houghton scored the winner with a header. He used to cut his own hair in the dressing room before a game so I'll give that one to him for that.

Do you have a favourite kit?

Good question... I think the 1994 World Cup kit – the white shirt with the green stripes coming down. And the Liverpool Candy kit – I'd have to say that. I wouldn't buy a kit now – only for my grandson.

What was your first pair of boots – and what was the best pair you've ever had?

Probably the old Stylo Matchmakers boots, the ones with the numbers on the side. The best pair was Nike. I always liked Nike. The coloured boots they wear these days aren't for me – I'm old fashioned.

Favourite pre-match meal back then and how do you prepare before you go on the radio now?

Chicken and beans when I played. Before the radio? Whatever... full brekkie!

Do you think it's right that some managers rest players for FA Cup ties? Do you think it devalues the competition?

I'd like to say no but the way it's gone know I can see why they do it. It's part and parcel of the game now.

Liverpool don't play that often on a Saturday anymore. What's your favourite and least favourite kick-off time?

My favourite kick-off time is 3pm on a Saturday. Worst is 8pm on a Monday night... or 4pm in London on a Sunday afternoon because I can't get back in time for my pint – that does my head in!

You used to own Aldo's Place bar in Liverpool city centre. How did you find running a bar?

It was a bad experience. I thought it was a good idea at the time but I was let down badly by people I thought I could trust. It's not something I will ever go in to again.

Do you have a pet?

Yeah – a German alsatian... who knows how to open doors on his own!

Why were England so bad at the World Cup? Do you care – or did you want them to lose?

It doesn't bother me how they do now. It reminded me of Liverpool last season (2009/10). There was no belief, no togetherness. It looked like they didn't want to fight for each other, there was no spirit.

Where were you when you heard that Steven Gerrard was going to Chelsea in 2005?

I was actually getting off a plane, coming back from Portugal. Sky met me with a camera at Manchester Airport. Obviously I was devastated but it turned out alright in the end. Him and Carra are Liverpool.

If they had to name a new stand after someone at Anfield, who would you pick?

Shankly. Without a shadow of a doubt.

Who was the best and worst at keepy-ups you have known?

The worst was probably me. The best? Probably Walshie (Paul Walsh).

What was the worst hangover you've ever had?

When I was at Oxford and went to Bangor in Northern Ireland for pre-season. We all stayed out to 3am thinking we were big men. Training the next day was not good. After the Christmas parties at Liverpool as well. I always remember training the next day after those nights out. It was part and parcel of the whole experience that you had to turn up for training and go through that – no matter how bad you were feeling.

How do you keep fit now?
I've got a gym upstairs and I go to the David Lloyd club four times a week. I think it's inbred in you. I enjoy it. My Dad had a big ale gut and he always used to say to me: 'You'll end up like me one day'. It was one of the best things he ever said to me because I made sure I didn't. It was a good bit of psychology from my Dad.

There was an idea a while ago about a football club being set up in Dublin. What do you think of that?
It would have been a great money-making venture. You only have to look at Sunderland. Roy Keane took over and Quinny (Niall Quinn) and they ended up being everyone's second team in the Republic. I think the idea would have got plenty of support.

Ever had a go at gaelic football?
No – but I think it is brilliant. I've been over to Croke Park and seen it – and the hurling. The players are so committed and they don't even get paid.

Would you ever move out of Liverpool?
The only place I would think of moving to would be Praia Da Luz in Portugal, where I've got my villa. But I can't see it. I will always have a house in Liverpool.

What's your ideal job in football?
Chief Scout at Liverpool Football Club. I just think that there's so much rubbish been brought in to the club over recent years that something should be done about it.

Who's the best player you've played with?
John Barnes.

Who's the best after-dinner speaker you've seen?
Geoff Miller – the England cricket chairman of selectors.

Who was your room-mate on away trips when you were a player? Who was the worst room-mate you ever had?
Ray Houghton – for Liverpool and Ireland. It more or less stayed the same throughout my career. Worst was Stevie Nicol – as much as I love him, I'd have to say that.

Who was the last footballer you heard from?
Probably Thommo (Phil Thompson) or Jason (McAteer). We all still keep in touch and meet up in the Carlsberg Lounge after the games at Anfield.

What was your best round of golf and where was your most enjoyable 18 holes?
Best was at Lee Park Golf Club near where I live – you can see the card at the start of this section. Most enjoyable was the Oceanico O'Connor Golf Club in Amendoeira, Portugal, which was designed by Christy O'Connor Junior.

Did you have any pre-match rituals when you were a player? Did any of the other players have any unusual habits or superstitions before a game?
The only one I had was that I liked to go out last when the team ran out. Phil Neal had an unusual superstition. He wouldn't put his shorts on until he had seen the 'This Is Anfield' sign. He'd come out of the dressing room in his boxer shorts and then put on his shorts once he'd seen the sign!

What music did the teams you played for listen to in the dressing room?
We didn't listen to music in those days. When I was Tranmere manager, we would listen to '70s soul music – much to the lads' dismay.

If the opportunity ever arose, would you go back into football management?
No.

What's the best footballer's autobiography you've read?
Paul McGrath's.

Who was the hardest working player in training sessions?
Tough one... I'd probably say Ray Houghton – he used to work his socks off.

Who was the hardest footballer you've known?
Paul (McGrath).

Do you play fantasy football?
No.

Where is the coldest you've ever been as a commentator? Can you ever remember getting soaked while you were doing the radio coverage?
Coldest was at Charlton five or so years ago – it was horrendous. I also remember at Newcastle when it lashed down and we got soaked – I ended up with a plastic bag on my head to keep the rain off! Apparently they've still got that picture on the Radio City website.

Have you ever owned a race horse?
Yeah – I've owned a couple. One that won twice for us and another one I owned with Stan (Steve Staunton). But we ended up losing £12,000 on that.

Ever refused to do an interview?
Yeah – you can probably guess which newspaper and why...

Do you think you're born to be a goalscorer? Is it different to other football positions?
I called it an illness – it was like an illness inside me that I was driven to score goals.

EITHER/OR

Kevin Keegan or Kenny Dalglish?
Kevin Keegan was my hero growing up but I think you've got to go with Kenny Dalglish for what he's done for the club.

BBC or ITV?
ITV.

Hurling or GAA (Gaelic football)?
Gaelic – just.

European Cup or League Title?
For Liverpool at the moment it has to to be the league title.

Shoes or trainers?
I prefer trainers.

Scoring at Anfield or scoring at Wembley?
Scoring at Anfield.

Red wine or white wine?
Red.

Saturday evening kick-off or Sunday afternoon?
Saturday evening.

Andy Gray or Clive Tyldesley?
Clive Tyldesley.

Hot holiday or skiing break?
Hot.

Igor Biscan or Bruno Cheyrou?
Biscan.

Main Stand or Centenary Stand at Anfield?
Main Stand.

Sunday Mirror or Sunday Times?
Mirror.

Cooked breakfast or cereal?
I love a cooked breakfast but I'll only have one at the weekend.

Studs or blades?
Studs.

Poor Scouser Tommy or Fields Of Anfield Road?
Poor Scouser Tommy.

Daniel Agger or Martin Skrtel?
Agger – just.

Half-time Bovril or soup?
Soup.

Lionel Messi or David Villa?
Messi.

1977 Rome or 1984 Rome?
Rome '77.

Europa League or League Cup?
Europa League.

Stevie in the centre or behind a striker?
Either... depends who the other players are... tough one.

Old league championship or Premier League trophy?
The old one, yeah.

Day at the races or sportsmen's dinner?
Have to be a day at the races.

Match programme or fanzine?
I'd probably go for the Kop Magazine – that's a good read.

Arsene Wenger or David Moyes?
David Moyes.

Adidas Tango or Nike Premier League ball?
Nike ball.

Standing Kop or seated Kop?
I loved the standing Kop but obviously after Hillsborough, things had to change.

Glass half-full or half-empty?
Half-full.

Tea or coffee?
A nice cup of tea.

Alan Hansen or Bobby Moore?
Bobby Moore.

Villa Park or St James's Park?
St James's Park.

Les Parry or Rick Parry?
Les Parry.

Superlambanana or Liver bird?
Liver bird.

Ring Of Fire or the Anfield Rap?
Ring Of Fire!

MY BESTS & WORSTS

**MY BEST LIVERPOOL XI SINCE I FIRST STARTED
WATCHING THE REDS IN 1967.**

Ray Clemence
I played against Ray in the latter part of his career. Even at that age he was still brilliant. Pepe Reina is a good keeper but Clem was just slightly better.

Phil Neal
There are a few options for this position, such as Jamie Carragher, but I have to go for Phil because he won more than anyone else in the club's history. He was a brilliant right back and a great penalty taker too.

Alan Hansen
We had a few tussles in training. Jockey was fantastic at the back and very difficult to replace. His departure was one of the reasons why the club started to struggle.

Tommy Smith
Would work very well alongside Jockey and not too many strikers, including me, would like to play against the pair of them.

Emlyn Hughes
He was simply a great player and has to be in the side, whether Smithy likes it or not.

Kevin Keegan
I can't put Keegan up front and I refuse to leave him out completely, so I'll put him on the right wing. What a player he was. I can still remember his debut against Nottingham

Forest, it was obvious that he was brilliant. Carlos Tevez is probably his modern day equivalent.

Graeme Souness

Nobody could impose themselves on a game better than Graeme. He just had the ability to grab it by the scruff of the neck and drive the team to victory.

Steven Gerrard

I think he just slightly surpasses Souness as a brilliant all-round midfielder. Graeme was special but he played in a great team. Stevie didn't have that around him, yet he has stood out for over a decade.

John Barnes

At his best nobody could stop him. He was the same as Cristiano Ronaldo has been at his best. The difference was he was more of a team player. He was the best player in our team, which is some accolade.

Kenny Dalglish

I saw his first game at Anfield, when he scored against Newcastle. He was tremendous. I've always been a closet Celtic fan so I already knew a lot about him. Seeing him in the flesh confirmed what I thought about his qualities.

Roger Hunt

As you know by now – my hero, and the first name on my teamsheet. He was the equivalent of what Fernando Torres is to the team now. Roger was the reason why I wanted to be a centre-forward.

Subs:

Pepe Reina (gk) Ian Rush, Robbie Fowler, Phil Thompson, Ian Callaghan.

MY BEST IRELAND XI

1. Given (GK)
2. Irwin (RB)
3. Mick McCarthy (CB)
4. Paul McGrath (CB)
5. Stan (LB)
6. Ray (Houghton – LM)
7. Keane (CM)
8. Whelan (CM)
9. Brady (LM)
10. Quinn (CF)
11. Robbie Keane (CF)

Subs: Packie Bonner (gk), Johnny Giles, Richard Dunne, Andy Townsend, Frank Stapleton.

MY BEST SCOUSE XI

1. Warner (GK)
2. Carra (RB/CB)
3. Smith (CB)
4. Thommo (CB)
5. Gerry Byrne (LB)
6. Terry Mc (CM)
7. Stevie G (CM)
8. Cally (LM)
9. Robbie (CF)
10. Me! (CF)
11. Jimmy Case (RM)

Subs: Frankie Lane (gk), Lawler, Sammy Lee, Davey Fairclough (supersub), David Johnson. Some of these players can play in different positions so this team is pretty flexible.

GERARD HOULLIER'S WORST LFC XI

1. Patrice Luzi
2. Abel Xavier
3. Jean Michel Ferri
4. Frode Kippe
5. Gregory Vignal
6. Harry Kewell
7. Igor Biscan
8. Bruno Cheyrou
9. Salif Diao
10. El Hadji Diouf
11. Djibril Cisse

When Gerard came back for the TNS Game in the summer of 2005, he was sitting in the directors' box. There was a fella sitting down below in the stand and he shouted up to him: "Thanks for the treble Gerard!" Houllier smiled and waved back at him and said: "No problem". Then the fella said: '"Yeah – Diao, Diouf and Cheyrou – now sod off!"

RAFA BENITEZ'S WORST LFC XI

1. Charles Itandje
2. Philipp Degen
3. Gabriel Paletta
4. Mauricio Pellegrino
5. Josemi
6. Antonio Nunez
7. Mark Gonzalez
8. Andrea Dossena
9. Sebastian Leto
10. Andriy Voronin (worst of the lot – he did my head in!)
11. Ryan Babel

WHAT THEY'VE SAID ABOUT ME
(Selected anecdotes and quotes)

'I'll never forget that match against Mexico at USA '94. I lost my head a bit and started throwing water bottles about the place. I wanted Aldo to come on as a substitute but this FIFA geezer was having none of it. Aldo started going mad to him in Spanish – hardly surprising since there were so many Mexicans around. As we both discovered later, Egyptian FIFA officials are not in the habit of speaking Spanish!'

– Former Ireland manager Jack Charlton

'When I was at Liverpool the fans took Aldo to their hearts because they knew he was one of their own, and the players all had a high regard for him both as a professional and as a person'

– Former Liverpool manager Kenny Dalglish

'His anticipation and eye for goal was outstanding. He had a terrific positional sense, was good in the air and a very cool penalty taker as well. I'm pleased and proud to think I inspired John as a kid on the Kop'

– 'Sir' Roger Hunt

'I remember going along to Aldo's dad's birthday party one Sunday night. The party was going with a real swing and I hit it off with Aldo's dad. He could play the spoons so he entertained a group of us and the drink was flowing to the extent that I quickly lost all track of time. It got too late for Aldo who said his farewells around midnight. It wasn't until 2.30am that I departed for home and when I reported for training about seven hours later, Aldo wasn't his usual chirpy self. But I was feeling fine and put in a good shift'

– Former LFC colleague John Wark

'I roomed with John Aldridge during my Liverpool days. He was great. He did so well to take over from Rushie – his goalscoring record was phenomenal, so full credit to John. He was a true athlete, a really fit lad. When we were on pre-season or away in a hotel he would come in after light training and carry on doing sit-ups and press-ups on the floor while I'd be flat out watching the telly. But as a room-mate he was a lazy sod. He never made the tea and I used to have to do all the running around and look after him. He used to love doing the crosswords. Is it any wonder he ended up playing to a ripe old age!'

– Nigel Spackman, former Liverpool colleague

'Aldo was never the quickest or the tallest but he was a great goalscorer. If you put the ball in the box nine times out of ten he'd be there to bury it. When you look at his record it was absolutely phenomenal, one of the best in British football ever. There are hundreds of stories I could tell you about Aldo, but I'd probably get both myself and him in trouble. The funniest that took place on the field was when Ireland went to play a game in Luxembourg. At the time Aldo still hadn't scored for us and it was obviously bothering him, even if we all found it hilarious. During the game the ball was knocked into the box and John tucked it away. He was so relieved to finally have done it that he immediately sprinted behind the goal to where the Ireland fans were. He started celebrating madly, pumping his fists. At the same time Ray Houghton and me were back in midfield screaming at Aldo to get back on the pitch and trying not to laugh at him. He hadn't realised that the goal had been disallowed for offside. He was going nuts celebrating while the game had continued'

**– Ronnie Whelan, former Liverpool
and Ireland colleague**

*(Acknowledgements: Wark On by John Wark, published by Know The Score Books;
The John Aldridge Testimonial Programme, Tranmere Rovers, May 1996)*

AFTER-DINNER TALES

(Some great stories I can remember from those I've seen)

Jan Molby

Jan was lining up to get his weight taken after the summer break. It was during Graeme Souness's time as manager.

They were going along the line with each of the players taking their turn to go on the scales and get their weight taken. They were getting close to the end and Souness looks down the line at Jan, who's put on a few pounds, and says: "It looks like you've had a good summer Jan". He asks: "What weight are you?" Jan says: "16 stone".

When it comes to his turn, Jan takes the short walk to the scales and his weight comes back as 17 stone 4 pounds.

Souness says: "Christ, Jan, what have you eaten from there to there?"

Jan usually starts his act by saying: "Before we go any further... 18 stone 5!" Because everyone is wondering what he weighs, he puts it to bed at the start and makes a laugh out of it. I'm not sure those weights I've quoted are accurate – but you get the idea!

Ronnie Whelan

Ronnie tells a really good story about when he first started at Liverpool. In his first game he did really well and scored a goal. The next game is against Manchester United.

It's a massive game, as it always is, plus Ronnie was a United fan when he was growing up and he has got a lot of family coming over for it.

So he goes in to see Bob Paisley who was in charge at the time and says: "Is there any chance I can have some extra tickets for Saturday's game?"

Bob says: "How many do you want?"

Ronnie replies: "five".

Paisley says: "You can have six – because you won't be bloody playing!"

That was the Liverpool way – Ronnie had played well but got left out the next game. That was Bob's way of keeping his feet on the ground.

Ron Yeats

He's on a train going to play his first game for Dundee and a fella gets on next to him with a bottle of whisky. He offers him a drink but big Ron says: "No, no, I'm playing football soon".

Later on he gets to the game. It's a freezing cold day and the pitch is frozen. Ron is the captain and goes up to the centre circle for the start of the game. He takes one look at the referee and realises it is the fella who was on the train with the whisky. He then flicks up the coin and tries to catch it but he misses it. He bends down to pick it up and he falls over.

Ron said that he looked after him throughout the game. He was fouling everyone left, right and centre but he let him get away with it – because he knew Ron knew who he was and that he'd had a bottle of Scotch before the match!

Tommy Smith

This is a famous tale about Shankly that you may have heard but it's one that Tommy tells well.

They are playing five-a-side and there is a dodgy decision. Shankly turns around and says to Chris Lawler, who is on the opposite side: "It was over the line, wasn't it?"

Chris, who was a quiet lad, replies: "I don't think so, gaffer".

Shankly says: "Bloody hell Chris, you've been here for a year and you haven't said a word and when you do open you mouth, it's a lie!"

My favourite Shankly story is from when Liverpool were playing against West-Ham in the mid-'60s.

Before the game, Shanks always used to watch the opposition pass by. As usual, he watches the West Ham players coming in to Upton Park and then he goes in to the visitors' dressing room and names the Liverpool side. He says: "Right, lads, here's the team that's going to win here today. You're going to win 5-0 and I'll tell you why.

"Martin Peters has just walked past me, white as a ghost, scared stiff of playing Liverpool Football Club... Geoff Hurst has walked past and he's limping... Bobby Moore's walked past and he's still pissed from the night before.

"When it gets to 5-0 lads, we're going to take our foot off the gas because we've got a big game next week, a much more important game than we've got today".

The game gets under way and Liverpool are winning not 5-0 but 5-1. Peter Thompson is running past the bench and he stops to have a word with Shankly. He asks: "Boss, shall I tell the lads to take their foot off the gas now?"

Shankly says: "No... humiliate the bastards!"

I think that's a brilliant story.

NUMBERS UP

Most goals in first 100 games for Liverpool Football Club in all competitions...

68: Roger Hunt
Sam Raybould
64: Jack Parkinson
61: John Aldridge
Albert Stubbins
Fernando Torres
56: Ian Rush
55: Robbie Fowler
Gordon Hodgson
49: Kenny Dalglish

CURRICULUM VITAE

NAME: John Aldridge, aka 'Aldo'
HEIGHT: 5ft 11ins
DATE OF BIRTH: 18.09.58
PLACE OF BIRTH: Liverpool
POSITION: Forward
NATIONALITY: Ireland
KOPITE: 1958-1978
LIVERPUDLIAN: Lifetime
MEDIA PUNDIT: 2001-present

PLAYING CAREER:
(Subs appearances in brackets)

SOUTH LIVERPOOL
(01.08.78-02.05.79)
No stats available

NEWPORT COUNTY
(02.05.79-21.03.84)
League appearances: 159 (11)
League goals: 69
FA Cup apps: 12 (1)
FA Cup goals: 7
League Cup: 11 (0)
League Cup goals: 5
Other appearances: 19 (0)
Other goals: 9

OXFORD UNITED
(21.03.84-27.01.87)
League appearances: 111 (3)
League goals: 72
FA Cup apps: 5 (0)

FA Cup goals: 2
League Cup: 17 (0)
League Cup goals: 14
Other appearances: 5 (0)
Other goals: 4

LIVERPOOL
(27.01.87-01.09.89)
League appearances: 69 (14)
League goals: 50
FA Cup apps: 12 (0)
FA Cup goals: 8
League Cup: 7 (1)
League Cup goals: 3
Other appearances: 1 (0)
Other goals: 2

REAL SOCIEDAD
(01.09.89-11.07.91)
League appearances: 63 (0)
League goals: 33
Other goals: 7

TRANMERE ROVERS
(11.07.91-31.05.98)
League appearances: 221 (21)
League goals: 138
FA Cup apps: 8 (1)
FA Cup goals: 4
League Cup: 25 (0)
League Cup goals: 22
Other appearances: 18 (0)
Other goals: 10

Manager: *1998-2001*
(Worthington Cup finalist 2000)

ALRIGHT ALDO

PLAYING RECORD, CLUB CAREER
(NEWPORT COUNTY – TRANMERE ROVERS, 1979-1998)

NEWPORT COUNTY

	Apps	Goals
League	170	69
FA Cup	13	7
League Cup	11	5
Other	19	9
TOTAL	*213*	*90*

OXFORD UNITED

	Apps	Goals
League	114	72
FA Cup	5	2
League Cup	17	14
Other	5	2
TOTAL	*141*	*90*

LIVERPOOL

	Apps	Goals
League	83	50
FA Cup	12	8
League Cup	8	3
Other	1	2
TOTAL	*104*	*63*

REAL SOCIEDAD

	Apps	Goals
League	66	33
Other	9	7*

* 6 Copa del Rey (Spanish cup), 1 UEFA Cup

TOTAL	75	40

TRANMERE ROVERS

	Apps	Goals
League	242	138
FA Cup	9	4
League Cup	25	22
Other	18	10

TOTAL	294	174

CAREER CLUB TOTAL

APPS	GOALS
827	457

PLAYING RECORD, INTERNATIONAL CAREER
(1986-1996)

REPUBLIC OF IRELAND

APPS	GOALS
58 (11)	19

IN A LIVERPOOL SHIRT

LEAGUE
Appearances	Goals
83	50

FA CUP
Appearances	Goals
12	8

LEAGUE CUP
Appearances	Goals
8	3

FA CHARITY SHIELD
Appearances	Goals
1	2

TOTAL
Appearances	Goals
104	63

LIVERPOOL GOALS

TOTAL (63)

LEAGUE (50)

5 – Charlton Athletic
4 – Luton Town, Newcastle Utd,
Nottingham Forest, Southampton.
3 – Coventry City, Derby County, QPR
2 – Arsenal, Chelsea, Middlesbrough, Oxford Utd,
Watford, West Ham Utd, Wimbledon.
1 – Crystal Palace, Manchester Utd, Millwall,
Portsmouth, Sheffield Wed, Tottenham Hotspur

FA CUP (8)
4- Nottingham Forest
2- Hull City
1- Everton, Millwall.

LEAGUE CUP (3)
1- Arsenal, Blackburn Rovers, West Ham Utd

FA CHARITY SHIELD (2)
2- Wimbledon.

THE 63 GOALS WERE SCORED AGAINST
8 – Nottingham Forest
5 – Charlton Athletic
4 – Luton Town, Newcastle Utd, Southampton, Wimbledon
3 – Arsenal, Coventry City, Derby County, QPR, West Ham Utd
2 – Chelsea, Hull City, Middlesbrough, Millwall, Oxford Utd, Watford
1 – Blackburn Rovers, Crystal Palace, Everton, Manchester Utd, Portsmouth, Sheffield Wed, Tottenham Hotspur

FASTEST TO 50 GOALS FOR LIVERPOOL (LEAGUE)

72 (games)	Fernando Torres	29.12.2009
80	Sam Raybould	1.11.1902
80	Albert Stubbins	22.1.1949
81	Roger Hunt	14.10.1961
82	Jack Parkinson	12.4.1909
83	John Aldridge	12.9.1989
84	Ian Rush	29.10.1983
88	Robbie Fowler	17.12.1995
90	Gordon Hodgson	27.10.1928
98	Harry Chambers	25.3.1922
98	Kenny Dalglish	10.11.1979
98	Michael Owen	26.8.2000
104	Joe Hewitt	29.2.1908
105	Ian St John	8.2.1964

MOST GOALS SCORED IN FIRST
50 LEAGUE GAMES FOR LIVERPOOL

	No of goals	Year of 50th (league game)
George Allan	40	1898
Jack Parkinson	35	1906
Tony Rowley	34	1957
Fernando Torres	33	2009
John Evans	33	1955
Jimmy Ross	33	1896
Jimmy Smith	32	1930
John Aldridge	31	1988
Dave Hickson	31	1961
Robbie Fowler	30	1994
Tom Reid	30	1929
Albert Stubbins	30	1947

MOST GOALS SCORED FOR LIVERPOOL
IN FIRST 50 LEAGUE STARTS

	No. of goals
George Allan	40
Fernando Torres	36
Jack Parkinson	35
John Aldridge	34
Tony Rowley	34
John Evans	33
Robert Robinson	33
Jimmy Ross	33
Jimmy Smith	32
Robbie Fowler	32
Dave Hickson	30
Tom Reid	30
Albert Stubbins	30

LIVERPOOL: RECORD OF PENALTY SCORERS

(Leading scorers*)

42 – Jan Molby
38 – Phil Neal
34 – Billy Liddell
22 – Tommy Smith
21 – Steven Gerrard
20 – Robbie Fowler
17 – John Aldridge
16 – Terry McDermott

(* Up to end of 2009/2010 season)

IN AN IRELAND SHIRT

Leading appearance makers:

Shay Given (1996-), Kevin Kilbane (1997-) – 103
Steve Staunton (1988-2002) – 102
Robbie Keane (1998 -) – 99
Niall Quinn (1986 - 2002) – 91
Tony Cascarino (1985-1999) – 88
Damien Duff (1998-), Paul McGrath (1985-1997) – 83
Packie Bonner (1981-1996) – 80
Ray Houghton (1986-1997) – 73
Liam Brady (1974-1990),
Kenny Cunningham (1996-2005) – 72
Kevin Moran (1980-1994), Frank Stapleton (1976-1990) – 71
Andy Townsend (1989-1997) – 70
John Aldridge (1986-1996) – 69
David O'Leary (1976-1993) – 68
Roy Keane (1991-2005) – 67
Ian Harte (1996-2003) – 64
Gary Breen (1996-2004) – 63

John O'Shea (2001-) – 62
Johnny Giles (1959-1979) – 59
Richard Dunne (2000-) – 58
Mick McCarthy (1984-1992) – 57
Don Givens (1969-1981), Denis Irwin (1990-1999) – 56
Chris Hughton (1979-1991), Steve Finnan (2000-),
Ronnie Whelan Jnr (1981-1995) – 53
Gary Kelly (1994-2002), Mick Martin (1971-1983),
Jason McAteer (1994-2004) – 52
Paddy Mulligan (1969-1979) – 50

IRELAND GOALS

Robbie Keane – 39
Niall Quinn – 21
Frank Stapleton – 20
John Aldridge, Tony Cascarino, Don Givens – 19
Noel Cantwell – 14
Gerry Daly – 13
Jimmy Dunne – 12*
Ian Harte – 11
Liam Brady, David Connolly, Roy Keane, David Kelly,
Clinton Morrison, Kevin Sheedy, Paddy Moore – 9
Dermot Curtis, Tony Grealish, Paul McGrath,
Steve Staunton, Kevin Doyle – 8
Arthur Fitzsimons, Alf Ringstead, Andy Townsend,
Kevin Kilbane, Damien Duff, Richard Dunne, Gary Breen – 7
Tommy Coyne, Ray Houghton,Con Martin, Andy McEvoy,
Kevin Moran – 6
*Includes pre-war goals

FIRST GOAL FOR IRELAND
19.10.1988: Republic of Ireland 4, Tunisia 0 (H)
(Friendly, Lansdowne Road). *(Full debut: 26.03.1986, Friendly,
Lansdowne Road, Republic of Ireland 0, Wales 1)*

FIRST HAT-TRICK FOR IRELAND
17.10.1990: Republic of Ireland 5, Turkey 0
(European Championship qualifier, Lansdowne Road)
Aldridge: 15 mins, 57 mins, pen 70 mins

GOALS RECORD YEAR BY YEAR

Year	Start	Sub	Goal
1986	7	0	0
1987	6	0	0
1988	8	0	1
1989	5	2	2
1990	8	1	3
1991	3	1	0
1992	5	4	5
1993	6	0	2
1994	4	2	4
1995	5	0	2
1996	1	1	0
Total	58	11	19

LAST 10 IRELAND GAMES IN WHICH ALDO SCORED

Date/Comp	H/A	Opposition/Res
11.10.1995		
EC Qualifier	H	Latvia 2-1
16.11.1994		
EC Qualifier	A	N Ireland 4-0
07.09.1994		
EC Qualifier	A	Latvia 3-0
24.06.1994		
World Cup Finals	N	Mexico 1-2
08.09.1993		
World Cup Qualifier	H	Lithuania 2-0

09.06.1993
World Cup Qualifier   A   Latvia 2-0
09.09.1992
World Cup Qualifier   H   Latvia 4-0
26.05.1992
World Cup Qualifier   H   Albania 2-0
25.03.1992
Friendly   H   Switzerland 2-1
17.10.1990
EC Qualifier   H   Turkey 5-0

WORLD CUP FINALS APPEARANCES

Ireland 1, England 1 (Cagliari, Italy) *11.06.1990*
Ireland 0, Egypt 0 (Palermo, Italy) *17.06.1990*
Ireland 1, Holland 1 (Palermo, Italy) *21.06.1990*
Ireland 0, Romania 0* (Genoa, Italy) *25.06.1990*
Ireland 1, Italy 0 (New Jersey, USA) *18.06.1994*
Ireland 1, Mexico 2 (Orlando, USA) *24.06.1994*
Ireland 0, Norway 0 (New Jersey, USA) *28.06.1994*

* (Ireland win on penalties)

CAREER HONOURS

League Division One championship medal (1987-88)
League Division Two championship medal (1984-85)
FA Cup winners' medal (1988-89)
League Cup winners' medal (1985-86)
FA Charity Shield winners' medal (1988)
Welsh Cup winners' medal (1979-80)
League Division One runners-up medal (1988-89)
FA Cup runners-up medal (1987-88)
Worthington Cup runner-up (2000)*

* As Tranmere manager

CAREER HAT-TRICKS

Tranmere Rovers (9)
Oxford United (5)
Newport County (4)
Liverpool (3)
Real Sociedad (0)

Total hat-tricks: 23

LIVERPOOL MEDIA

(During the time Aldo worked as media pundit,
starting from UEFA Cup final for Radio 5, 2001)

LIVERPOOL FC HONOURS
UEFA Cup – 2000/01
European Super Cup – 2001/02, 2005/06
Worthington Cup – 2002/03
Champions League – 2004/05
Champions League finalist – 2006/07
FA Cup – 2005/06
FA Community Shield – 2001, 2006

(* Stats up to date as of August 2010)

Stats compiled by Ged Rea and Dave Ball

INDEX

Other Sport Media titles

Cally On The Ball
50 short tales from the
man who's had a
marathon love affair
with Liverpool FC

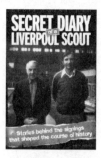

Secret Diary of a
Liverpool Scout
Story of Shankly's Chief Scout
Geoff Twentyman and the stars
he discovered

Liverpool FC
Banners
The ultimate fans'
collection

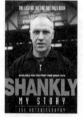

Shankly: My Story
The one and only
autobiography of the
Kop messiah

Oh I Am A
Liverpudlian And I
Come From The
Spion Kop
Celebrating football's
most iconic stand

The Kop
Popular unofficial
monthly fans'
magazine

**All of these titles, and more, are available to order by calling
0845 143 0001 or you can buy online at www.merseyshop.com**

Alright Aldo